I couldn't put this book down. I found myself squeezing in a chapter or a page as often as I could throughout my days, feeling as though it were water in a desert, feeling my heart rate slow and my mind rest and my soul become renewed. Sara beautifully reflects God's heart throughout these pages, calling us to come, to be curious, to be gentle with ourselves as we learn to settle into God's pace and His goodness in our lives, no matter our story or pains. This is a must-read for any believer.

—ALYSSA BETHKE, author, *Satisfied* and
When Doing It All Is Undoing You

After reading part 1 of Sara's book I sat and wept. Finally—words to feelings that I have not been able to describe. This book has been healing, eye opening, and such a blessing to my life. We all *need* to read this book.

—ALEXA PENAVEGA, actress; author; producer

Written with vulnerable honesty and hard-won wisdom, Sara Hagerty's beautiful book unpacks the hopeful reality that our hearts can rest, and even come alive, within the boundaries around them. Sara unpacks the uncomfortable truth that all of us have limitations, and it is within them that we are invited to come to God honestly and there flourish in His love. I love this book and am so deeply encouraged by what it unveils.

—STASI ELDREDGE, bestselling author, *Captivating*

This book is a lyrical masterpiece. Every paragraph reads like a poem, captivating in its truth and beauty. So many books tell us we can do more and be more; Sara suggests spiritual health may be found when we accept less and perhaps even do less. Rather than seeing our limitations as something to overcome, she eloquently makes the case that our limitations aren't just gifts from God but a reflection of God in the flesh. Beautiful.

—GARY THOMAS, teaching pastor, Cherry Hills Community
Church, Highlands Ranch, Colorado; author, *Sacred
Marriage*, *Cherish*, *Sacred Pathways*, and *Thirsting for God*

If you find yourself wishing things were like they used to be, longing for what could have been, or hoping for a change in what lies ahead, Sara's is the voice you need. She puts words to the inner cry of a burdened heart, articulating what we all know but can't accept: we are limited, and we wish we weren't. This book will lift your eyes to the goodness of the boundaries we didn't choose and show you how to live fully behind your fences.

—PHYLICIA MASONHEIMER, founder and
CEO, Every Woman a Theologian

"God has a purpose in our limits." As a woman called to share the gospel in the "get better, faster, and stronger" world of health and fitness, I wish someone had taught me this kind of head-scratching, wonderful truth. My aging body wishes it knew then, when it was younger, what Sara is teaching us now. In this book, Sara does what she does best: give us cause to see a limitless God and His wonderous ways while feeling normal when constrained by endless piles of laundry, missing socks, and lost dreams. By the time your fingers turn the last page, you will know God's kindness in what appears to be weak and out of reach.

—ALISA KEETON, founder, Revelation Wellness;
bestselling author, *The Body Revelation*

Even before I read the first word of this book, I began recommending it, because I know Sara. Her vocabulary reminds me of my mentor and hero, Elisabeth Elliot, who also used the words surrender, loss, and gift. Like her, Sara has walked through deep waters and, by not rushing ahead, has discovered more of God in the murky darkness. This book is an invitation to live in the messiness of losses and to find there the surprising joy of Immanuel, God with you, giving you gifts in your limitations. Like Sara, this book is a rich, deep well. Be fed. Be nourished.

—BARBARA RAINEY, author; artist; mom
to six; "Mimi" to twenty-seven

Sarah has the rare gift of sharing, with brutal honesty, her own struggles while leading us gently into both the mystery and the surprising joy that limitations can bring into our lives. Her book brought me into a new place of resting in God's arms. I treasured every word.

—SUSAN ALEXANDER YATES, speaker; blogger; bestselling author, *Risky Faith*, *The One Devotional*, and *Cousin Camp*

Through masterful storytelling, Sara helps us see how a limitation is actually an invitation to experience God's presence and provision in a profound way. After reading this beautiful book, you will no longer see the constraints in your life as things that grievously hold you back but rather as gifts that graciously hold you within the boundary lines of God's best for you. Sara shows us it is truly possible to embrace our limitations and live freely and fully in God's love within them.

—JEANNIE CUNNION, bestselling author, *Mom Set Free* and *Don't Miss Out*

With a deft and discerning hand, Sara Hagerty uses beautiful prose to paint for us the landscape of our lives. Which of us can honestly say that our days are not filled with stuff we would never choose for ourselves? And yet Sara gently helps us view life's roadblocks, setbacks, heartbreaks, and hardships—our limitations—from the divine perspective. No matter your challenges or season of life, I believe you'll find new hope and genuine encouragement throughout this book. It certainly deeply impacted me.

—LISA JACOBSON, founder, Club31Women

What would it look like to believe—truly believe—that the boundary lines of your life have fallen in pleasant places? With the wisdom of a seasoned tour guide and the empathy of a trusted friend, Sara Hagerty takes us by the hand and shows us how to exchange our thoughts and ideals for God's so that, instead of being a burden, our limitations become a wonder—a wonder-full part of our stories. Sara is one of the most gifted writers of our day, and this is the transformational book your soul has been longing to read.

—JODIE BERNDT, bestselling author, Praying the Scriptures series

This book cracked my soul wide open and gave words to the unnamed but ever-present longings of my heart in this season. This book is for the dreamers, the fixers, the goal setters. This one is for the ever-hopeful and the cynic alike. This one is for all of us who are longing for a deeper look at His face and His heart. Sara gently asks the prodding questions that my heart needed to be drawn closer to Him. She is a wise guide on our journey deeper into His heart.

—KATIE DAVIS MAJORS, bestselling author;
founder, Amazima Ministries

THE
GIFT of
LIMITATIONS

THE

GIFT *of*

LIMITATIONS

FINDING BEAUTY
in YOUR BOUNDARIES

SARA HAGERTY

ZONDERVAN
BOOKS

ZONDERVAN BOOKS

The Gift of Limitations
Copyright © 2024 by Sara Hagerty

Published in Grand Rapids, Michigan, by Zondervan. Zondervan is a registered trademark of The Zondervan Corporation, L.L.C., a wholly owned subsidiary of HarperCollins Christian Publishing, Inc.

Requests for information should be addressed to customercare@harpercollins.com.

Zondervan titles may be purchased in bulk for educational, business, fundraising, or sales promotional use. For information, please email SpecialMarkets@Zondervan.com.

ISBN 978-0-310-35704-9 (hardcover)
ISBN 978-0-310-35707-0 (audio)
ISBN 978-0-310-35706-3 (ebook)

Unless otherwise noted, Scripture quotations are taken from The Holy Bible, New International Version®, NIV®. Copyright © 1973, 1978, 1984, 2011 by Biblica, Inc.® Used by permission of Zondervan. All rights reserved worldwide. www.Zondervan.com. The "NIV" and "New International Version" are trademarks registered in the United States Patent and Trademark Office by Biblica, Inc.®

Scripture quotations marked AMP are taken from the Amplified® Bible (AMP). Copyright © 2015 by The Lockman Foundation. Used by permission. www.lockman.org

Scripture quotations marked ESV are taken from the ESV® Bible (The Holy Bible, English Standard Version®). Copyright © 2001 by Crossway, a publishing ministry of Good News Publishers. Used by permission. All rights reserved.

Scripture quotations marked Message are taken from *THE MESSAGE*. Copyright © 1993, 2002, 2018 by Eugene H. Peterson. Used by permission of NavPress. All rights reserved. Represented by Tyndale House Publishers, Inc.

Scripture quotations marked NASB are taken from the New American Standard Bible® (NASB). Copyright © 1960, 1962, 1963, 1968, 1971, 1972, 1973, 1975, 1977, 1995 by The Lockman Foundation. Used by permission. www.lockman.org

Scripture quotations marked NKJV are taken from the New King James Version®. Copyright © 1982 by Thomas Nelson. Used by permission. All rights reserved.

Scripture quotations marked NLT are taken from the Holy Bible, New Living Translation. © 1996, 2004, 2015 by Tyndale House Foundation. Used by permission of Tyndale House Publishers, Inc., Carol Stream, Illinois 60188. All rights reserved.

Any internet addresses (websites, blogs, etc.) and telephone numbers in this book are offered as a resource. They are not intended in any way to be or imply an endorsement by Zondervan, nor does Zondervan vouch for the content of these sites and numbers for the life of this book.

All rights reserved. No part of this publication may be reproduced, stored in a retrieval system, or transmitted in any form or by any means—electronic, mechanical, photocopy, recording, or any other—except for brief quotations in printed reviews, without the prior permission of the publisher.

Published in association with Yates & Yates, www.yates2.com.

Cover design: James W. Hall IV
Cover photo: Wirestock Creators / Shutterstock
Interior design: Sara Colley

Printed in the United States of America

23 24 25 26 27 LBC 5 4 3 2 1

To Elizabeth, Befhers, Beth

We thought we were limitless when we were sixteen and full of dreams, didn't we? I'm so glad we each received stories that weren't the ones of our dreams but better. Here's to ten years of dreaming wildly and another twenty where we lived small, hedged in, and found Him to be wildly big.

Your friendship has given me endurance to find Him in my limitations.

Remember my chains.

—Colossians 4:18

Contents

Part 1

INSIDE THE FENCE LINE
Seeing Our Limits

OUR LIMITATIONS ARE OFTEN INVISIBLE BUT UNYIELD-ing fences in our lives until we are forced to notice them. These first few chapters are a guide to help you see the wire fence—the limitations you've been resenting or working fiercely to overcome, often subconsciously. Perhaps you'll also find the relief that comes when you name the invisible but powerful.

May we begin to see what God can do with what we resent. And to consider: might there be a purpose in these limits?

The Ache underneath Our Limits

In a game of chess you can make certain arbitrary concessions to your opponent, which stand to the ordinary rules of the game as miracles stand to the laws of nature. You can deprive yourself of a castle, or allow the other man sometimes to take back a move made inadvertently. But if you concede everything that at any moment happened to suit him—if all his moves were revocable and if all your pieces disappeared whenever their position on the board was not to his liking, then you could not have a game at all. So it is with the life of souls in a world: fixed laws, consequences unfolding by causal necessity, the whole natural order, are at once limits within which their common life is confined and also the sole condition under which any such life is possible.

—C. S. Lewis, *The Problem of Pain*

"IT ALL FEELS TOO MUCH."

A friend put words to feelings I'd felt but not named, and they ricocheted in my head for not just hours but weeks.

It *is* too much.

Too much laundry and too many bills. Too many dust bunnies in the corners and tabs open in my browser. Too many Amazon boxes and too much clutter. Too many mismatched socks. The backdrop to this is too much drama, too much crisis—too much to watch in the world in a day, much less pay attention to in my heart in an hour.

Somehow my world has become too much, too. Maybe I'm too much for me.

Responsible for too much and yet desirous of much more than what I have.

You see, I live limited.

My teenagers share their hearts just before my eyelids weigh shut at the end of the day, and my toddlers wake with the sun. We have seven children, but my arms held only three in their infancy. Our home is overwhelmed by stories, four that began outside our home.

These big stories and this enormous responsibility sew me into the hem of the world: all of us carrying too much. Mothers with sick children, sons with sick parents, single women looking under the hoods of their cars for the problem, dads juggling three jobs, and moms moonlighting to pay the bills. Financially secure ones eking out every one of their free minutes in philanthropy for the broken of the world. (Money or lack thereof doesn't ensure insulation from *it all feels too much*.) Friends bringing meals to hurting neighbors but themselves soaking their pillows with hidden tears and settling for fast food on their tables.

It all feels too much.

But the ache we feel—is it because we're carrying too much? Or is it because our responsibilities are large and our longing supersedes those responsibilities and causes us irreconcilable pain?

We humans pine. We were made to pine.

We all live inside a plot of life surrounded by a fence. Life inside the fence feels full and overwhelming, yet life on the other side appears expansive and open ended. We can all look outside our kitchen windows or our third-story flats and see our fence lines. We can see the places where our spaces end and the world beyond begins.

Wide eyed, we fantasize about more, but not more of the full life we already carry. More restraint-free living. That's what we want! A more that requires less.

We want to be untethered in our dreams. Reaching and then receiving. We want to live a *finally*.

But children wake us in the night before the morning we're hosting the party, or we roll our ankle before the big race. Sickness interrupts the family's dream trip, and the check doesn't clear before the registration fee is due. We grow more wrinkles, find more grey, and add more pounds each year, yet we lack what we want more of.

We live in the tension of too much and not enough. Belly bloated.

This hem of the world that ties us into one narrative is now also the ache of our want, the discomfort that we think comes from our limits. Surely relief comes when the fence line is moved.

Today was like most days at 9:36 or 9:32 or 9:41 in the morning. I suited up my littlest ones for a walk through the nature preserve that borders our house. This process is simple on sunny spring days when it's already sixty degrees, but this morning needed rain boots and raincoats—things that, no matter how many systems I put into place in our home, seem to lose themselves.

One pair of boots was already soaked, sitting outside in the rain. Living out in the country, my little kids spend most of their days in rain boots—fording creeks and walking muddy paths—or barefoot. I wondered, as I discovered this pair all askew on our lawn, how many rain boots have been discarded in the woods. And though our sock bin holds about a thousand socks, none seem to pair in size and color. Most days, I aim for just one of those two qualities to match.

What felt like thirty minutes later, we were out the door, disheveled but dressed, and exploring for signs of spring—an idealistic exploration for a wet and cold March. One of my three littles was quite rainy on the inside, and the wind chapped our cheeks. And our fingers. I forgot gloves. Wasn't it rainy, not cold? But, oh no, March confounds. I knew that if we headed back inside early, I'd have a few extra minutes to fill out the passport renewal form I wanted to finish. Nothing would be missed of this wet day, and we'd have more time, and time is currency for us adults. Taking a mediocre walk in dismal weather or chipping away at a never-ending task list when I was already chasing the clock: it was an obvious choice.

Except these days, I'm seeing that making sense—of my life, of my time, of my limits—is overrated. Enough years spent trying to make sense of a world I didn't make and that makes a stranger of me, and I have decided, with my mind and with my life, to distrust many of my unexamined instincts.

So on we walked through drizzle and puddles in a world that mainly was still brown.

And as we did, Charlotte absentmindedly sang "You Are My Sunshine," stringing words together, mumbling through the chorus. I knew what she was singing only because she'd sung it a dozen times the day before. The sky bulged with gray as if it might open up and turn from a drizzle to drench us, no promise of the spring sun. But her voice was like smelling salts awakening me to a reality I couldn't apprehend with my five senses. I couldn't see it if I was trying to make sense of my day or of my life. She sang my heart soft. I didn't forget the mismatched socks, the missing boots, or the seventeen minutes it took to get ready for this twenty-five-minute walk, but those encumbrances just felt less defining.

Bo looked for tadpoles along the muddy path, sloshing his rain boots mindlessly, spraying mud onto the back of his pants and coat, and informed me that the bird call I was sure came from a crow was that of a blue jay. Virginia's boots went *squerch squerch squerch* through the waterlogged path. This wasn't Christmas, when all was good and right; they argued some as we walked, scolding and tattling as young hearts are prone to do. I wouldn't write a poem about this day or even snap a picture to send to the grandparents. It wouldn't make our end-of-the-year family photo album. But it represented something, a hairline change of heart as strong as bone, but not visible. This walk represented God's presence growing into my awareness and my thinking.

To fully understand, you'd have to flash back to a day fifteen years earlier. Same girl, same March weather confusion, different surroundings. The boundary then was my body. Bellies of women around me expanded, signs of a family life from which I was excluded. Their lives grew while I stood fenced inside infertility, inside the *not yet, maybe never*. Years, then a decade, passed. Surely the wall around me was cement, not flimsy and easily overturned by a few desperate pleas in prayer but fortified. Definitive. I couldn't scale it, no matter the intention, no matter the intercession. That girl would have danced assuredly among mismatched socks and toddler-tattling. She wanted nothing more than the family.

She knew her limits with sharp, painful intimacy. Every month, every baby shower, every birth announcement, and every first birthday party reminded her of what she had tried so hard to forget. Every celebration pointed out the kitchen window to her fence line. She knew her limits almost better than she knew anything else.

She was also the girl who, just a few short years later, woke up one day into a world without her dad. She may have been thirty and independent, but even then, the loss of a father makes the world wobbly. Life limited her yet again. She was limited to one parent. One grandfather, now, for her future children. She was limited to the input and advice that only a mother can give, not the collective input from a mother and father. She was limited to being fatherless.

Though our landscapes change, the tight-chested feeling of always reaching for what is out of reach, deeply desiring what may be impossible, stretches across our seasons, stages, and circumstances. Round bellied and barefoot, or ringless without a plus one; not enough hours to work, not enough hours to play: our limits vary, but the tension between *it's all too much* and *it's just not enough* is often the same.

So that humdrum story of our rainy March walk without a spring bud isn't what it appears.

I never had a bin for socks before I had this many children. I keep my pairs neat and tightly folded. I don't lose things. I have a place for almost every one of my things. I don't lose *my* rain boots, and I can usually get out the door in three minutes or less. We'll track more mud back into the mudroom after one walk than I would have over years of walks by myself. So much of this picture is of a small life limited by nubby fingers that can't pull a zipper and by wandering feet, minds, and songs. It's full of too many mismatched socks and toddler complaints, and way too much rain gear. It's too much of what I wouldn't want and not enough of that for which I long.

This picture is of a girl—she'll always be a little girl. But she's growing. She has learned that every plot of land—every big city flat, every small-town suburban lot, every country acreage—has a border, a boundary. Every person has a fence line, yet that girl has ceased spending her afternoons digging underneath it or trying to climb over it.

She still wonders at the world on the other side, but the grass between her toes and the edge of the willow tree that now nearly touches the ground and brushes her ankles hold the most wonder. Her fence line isn't merely the marker of what isn't, what she can't have, can't do, or what is out of reach. Her fence line is a signpost directing her attention toward what's inside it. She has found something inside of it that makes it worth staying.

Mostly.

And yet some days, the fence still catches her eye, and it's all she can do not to dig her fingers into the dirt underneath it and shimmy her way out. Muscle memory of so many years of digging.

She's you. And she's me. Fickle-hearted with eyes that dart. Unsure of what's real. Forgetting. And then remembering.

The pages ahead are for remembering where we started and honoring where we find ourselves today—for finding life and exhilaration within the boundary lines God has given us, for finding Him right where we are, within the fence line.

The Psalm 16:6 reality that "the boundary lines have fallen for me in pleasant places" isn't yet our reality. We live in the friction of wanting more and yet also being overwhelmed with what already is. We're not quite sure, as the psalmist says, that we have "a beautiful inheritance" (ESV).

So we waffle. And we forget. And we study the fence line and what's on the other side more than we fall into the tall, silky grass of the field we've been given, expecting a soft landing.

We live with the strange juxtaposition of never having had more visibility into the wider world, and yet finding that the line between God's responsibility and ours—though hazy—hasn't changed in thousands of years. Our eyes dart between our finitude—our humanity—and the myth of our culture that we can be in more than one place at once and have it all.

These pages are your invitation to look at what you lack—to name your limitations—with the intention of becoming more His (and more yourself) in the midst of them, not in spite of them.

All of us—you, me, your neighbor, my neighbor—live in the tension of *too much, but not enough*, and I believe there's a day ahead for us when the fence line looks the same but our hearts are different. Our hearts are alive. They know where to turn when the fence line catches their attention. They know their maker and they rest where they are.

We all know what we can do. My friend knows how much a paycheck can cover for braces for many mouths. My neighbor knows how the city can thwart his intent to subdivide (and prevent him from building another home on his spacious property). My teenager knows her curfew and minimum wage. I know how little I can travel with a near-babe at home and how few girls' weekends I can take while raising seven. I know how few pages I can read or write with so many hearts to tend.

My friend with an autoimmune disease knows what she can't eat during a flare-up, and another who has a child with special needs knows how long her child can endure a playdate before she unravels. Another knows how many weekends she can travel to visit grandkids before she's lost her home base—*there are only fifty-two weeks in a year, you know.* The house is too small for large parties, or the yard too overgrown (not enough time to tend or prune) for the long-dreamed-of English garden. The budget is too tight for dinner out.

You are kept from what I have, and I can't have what you have. I want your quiet afternoons and your free evenings, and you want my arms full of family. Your meticulously maintained lawn is the dream of the tired landowner who has the sunsets you wished you could see if your neighbor's roof weren't in the way. The adventure-seeking friend you envy, whose passport is full of stamps, dreams at night that she could come home to your family.

And this hem of the world that ties us into one narrative is the ache of our want, the ache of our limits.

We all know our boundaries. If I asked you yours, they'd roll off your tongue. We study them in the recesses of our minds, in the free minutes of our day. Some of us sweat to scale the fence around us, and others fall at the feet of it, defeated before they try. Some of us do both. We live boundaried, and we know it even as we push against the limits. How we handle this life—these demands, these responsibilities, and even these joyful tasks—the *too much, but not quite enough* is our conundrum.

We live mostly dissatisfied, bloated by the vaporous nature of *too much*, but reaching for what's being served at the next table over.

"I have seen a limit to all perfection," the psalmist tells us (Ps. 119:96 ESV).

The psalmist, like us, is hemmed, seeing life's limits, where it all gets margined.

And I wonder: hemmed and frustrated forever? Hedged.

Contained. Drooling over the fence line, with one eye on our *too much* and another on what's not for the taking. Is this our lot?

Filled up by too much of not enough?

In my twenties, I lived as if I coauthored my stories with God. Now I keep stumbling into them, almost as if I read the last few pages first and then started the book to find the narrative.

A frigid, snowy January night held one of those stories.

The four of our children we adopted hold life and years of loss within their frames, and few other than their closest friends will ever know the depths. Their loss has threatened their future. Hope can feel like a cosmic joke when the world breaks before you turn five. Regardless of age, loss threatens to subtract from biblical hope.

Because of this, looking at the days ahead with laughter (Prov. 31:25) has always been a challenge in our home. And it was not until it became apparent that it was a challenge for them that I realized it was also a challenge for me. To hope for the future requires being able to feel secure in the present, confident in what He has for you in this present moment. Present in the present, even.

When our oldest showed an interest in our hosting an art show for her and her art instructor, it was an early sign that her hope might be restored one day. Could this show—a debut of the art she has been creating in the corners and shadows of her world and ours—indicate a healing thread within her?

We rallied to the idea. We plotted—inviting friends, securing musicians and food and decor. The show was scheduled for just after Christmas, not far enough away to fear, project the worst, rehearse it all falling apart, as children with broken histories often do. There were prints to make, finishing touches to put on her art, a website to update.

In the flurry, I'd proofread the invitations and the website and the emails sent to friends but not spent a moment considering the name that our daughter and her instructor chose for this night: "Far Better Things." It came from this quote by C. S. Lewis (one of our daughter's favorite authors): "There are far better things ahead than any we leave behind."[1]

The morning before the show, I sat in the dark winter quiet that fresh snow brings, warming my feet by the fire and acting, for a few hours at least, as if this were a typical weekend for us. Family and friends had come in from out of town, and we were hours away from the hustle required to make our daughter's night peaceful and smooth. It felt a bit like the morning of her wedding might—anticipation laced with what-ifs, thrill sitting under the weight of a list of tasks. I thought of this child we knew on paper before we'd met and how we'd prayed for her when all we'd known was her picture and her name and a few grainy videos sent to us from a friend with poor internet service and limited electricity, and I was reminded that hope is elusive to the orphaned heart. A theory. An idea. It's easier to keep the deeper things of God in idea form than to invite them to invade the fortresses we've built to protect ourselves from risk.

Then I remembered the name she'd selected for the show.

In this name, we sowed the reality we all so desperately want to believe but seems only the work of movies. We cite the Scripture verse about His plans and future for us, but we hedge our bets and live as our own landlords, monitoring and managing the property lines.

---

1. C. S. Lewis, *The Collected Letters of C. S. Lewis*, Volume 3: *Narnia, Cambridge, and Joy, 1950–1963* (San Francisco: HarperOne, 2007).

But a life fixed on too much of what we don't want or not enough of what we so deeply desire keeps us from God-inspired expectancy. Proverbs describes a woman who laughs at the days to come. She is expectant. To have this posture, to believe that "there are far better things ahead than any we leave behind," requires a present mind that isn't determined to overcome our limitations, isn't fixed on them.

The art show was majestic. Despite a surprising winter gale and an illness that spread like wildfire, droves of friends feasted that night—eyes on her otherworldly art, hearts full of His story, strings as the backdrop. I absorbed all the details of that night, and I watched her do the same, a slow and steady understanding dawning on her as she lived in that moment the hope of better days.

This kind of presence of mind does that. We start to expect that what is within reach, not what is out of reach, is going to be good. *So good.*

The future looks different from this perspective.

Noticing how the sun hits the crown of my baby girl's head in spring, tasting how caramelized onions make a dish that much better, pausing to hear the toddler singing two aisles over—it's as if by noticing and experiencing these things I'm reflecting that I can be right here in this moment because I know who He is and who I am, where the end of me meets the beginning of Him. Trust creates a powerful ability to be present, and being present to the small moments reinforces the trust that enabled it.

Letting a chill run up my spine as I sit in one line of poetry; savoring a text from a friend who has just spoken about something my heart struggles to see; staying too long in the flickering candlelight as the waitstaff closes down the restaurant—could being present to all of these moments be the holy small that reflects the peace that comes when I trust?

And trust eclipses the fence line. It doesn't eradicate it but casts a light that makes our experience of it different.

But the world doesn't teach me to trust.

With its gadgets and apps, the world has told me that I am limitless. That I can circumvent every obstacle, simplify the hard things, and bound over what confines me. That I can watch my daughter's ballet performance online while I saute onions on the stove and order a Christmas gift for a friend out of state. I can filter my wrinkles—alter the limits of youthfulness I keep butting up against with each birthday—and order my groceries while I pump my gas. I can scan Pinterest for sixteen ideas for a birthday party, forgetting that I have time to implement only one or two. Time is no longer the limit it once was. (Or is it?) The problem is that even as the world says I'm limitless, nothing has changed within me to make good on that promise. All of these new conveniences just enable me to bypass the boundaries, encourage my fingers to claw at the dirt under the fence line, to hope for a way—any way—through or under or over.

The limits can stay the same for a decade, but my way of relating to them can change. *I* can change in the same house, flat, or postage-stamp property with a fence line.

The psalmist tells us of this dance of living limited within ourselves, but thrusting our craving for limitlessness onto Him. "I have seen a limit to all perfection" (Ps. 119:96 ESV). But "your commandment is exceedingly broad *and* extends without limits" (AMP).

Aha! He is what you and I crave when we study the fence, when we look far into the distance. We are searching for those "far better things ahead."

And our daughter's art show was exactly that. Friends came in from the cold, held plates of food and laughed and cried and wrapped around her and her tucked-away talent, stood in front of small pieces of heart and story, like sea glass weathered by waves and torrents, but brilliant, mounted on the walls. It is a night I hold as if in a snow globe, available to pull off the shelf and stare at in wonder on the hard days and the dull-drum afternoons. And a night also filled with this God-infused promise: and still better to come, better ahead.

There is a limitlessness, an answer to the bubbling-over desire for what we don't have. A response to the too much of what we don't want but not enough of what we crave. An answer that makes the grass underneath our feet Lincoln green and incandescent under the sun.

But to receive it, to walk in it, to climb the black chestnut within our property lines and smell the honeysuckle, to stop to take in the summer-sweat curls against our baby's face rather than count the hours until bedtime, we have to take a closer look at the fence line, to notice our responses to it, to look for where He has been in it, to see what the world is saying about it.

What if this fence line is protecting me and you?

What if it's a gift? A deposit, directing our eyes to the now and to the far better things ahead?

——— *For Your Continued Pursuit* ———

Psalm 16:6 | Psalm 23:1–3 | Psalm 63:1 | Psalm 119:96 | Psalm 121:7–8 | Proverbs 31:25 | John 17:6 | Acts 17:26 | 2 Corinthians 4:17–18 | Philippians 3:20 | 1 Peter 2:11

This section at the end of each chapter is for readers who, like me, want to dig deeper by tracing what they read back to God's truth. Some verses are cited within each chapter and others are alluded to. I invite you to use these passages as starting points for dialogue with God about the limitations He has allowed in your life and for finding His eyes on you, there.

2

THE GIFT OF LIMITS

Suffering is not the opposite of blessing.
—EDMUND CLOWNEY, *THE MESSAGE OF 1 PETER*

WE JOINED A NEW BODY OF BELIEVERS, AND DOING SO came with new gatherings, new potential friends, and new *let me tell you my story's*. Once a week, we circled up: the moms launching kids alongside the ones who just tucked their babes in bed, bumping elbows with the single women, the empty nesters, and newly marrieds. It was a weekly night of sharing hearts.

This meeting started at the beginning of lacrosse season, when my boys and my husband lined the sidelines and played the field. It came just before our next round of teenagers started driving, but after they filled their social calendars. It came when toddlers weren't sleeping and my oldest was graduating. Despite how beautiful I kept hearing it was, there was no room to squeeze in this meeting and not squeeze out my soul.

I had waited for years to be one of the mothers in a group like this, one of the women proudly sharing about a child's growth or tearfully asking for prayer through a hard patch. To find myself finally in the thick of that dream come true only to realize that I no longer had the capacity to engage with small groups the way I used to was disorienting. It was a brand-new season, but it felt familiar deep in my bones. Whether we're limited by barrenness or by *too much*—too many bedtimes and hungry mouths and "Mom, can you listen to my recital pieces?"—this feeling isn't discriminatory, and it comes in all sorts of ways.

One of many *yet agains* where I stood on the other side of the window looking in—similar to the days when there just wasn't a way to reach what was on the other side.

Every one of us has a fence line. A "nope, you can't cross this line" set of circumstances in our lives. Some of us get especially adept at climbing, hurdling, and drilling holes in what won't budge to see if we can't break free. Like our puppy who scratched and chewed our brand-new carpet to escape the room where she was confined, most of us (passively, subtly) see our fence lines as captivity.

Fence lines appear shifty, sometimes moving in different seasons, but always present. I was fenced out by my infertility and, a mere decade later, fenced in by too many needs in my home.

But this sharp contrast showed me that I needn't always relate to my limits in the same way. I wished I could be a part of this sisterhood at our new church, formed around story, hunger for God, and a unique moment in time. It reminded me of my old wish to join the sisterhood formed around stretch marks, late-night feedings, and the whiplash of new motherhood. My muscle memory wanted to rehearse what I was missing, how I got there, to study possible ways around or through this fence. My thoughts taunted me, telling me that my story had always been one of chutes and ladders—never quite moving far enough up before quickly landing in a downward swoop. *Surely,* my thoughts said, *you must find a way to hurdle this fence and get to the other side.*

I paused, remembering my different relationship with the fence now. I had discovered the soft, enveloping feel of grass in my toes and the mystery of the roots of trees that shot up within my yard. I'd grown accustomed to the sound of the mourning dove and the wind whistling through the woods that lined the back of our house, the woods that lined my world. Wonder comes with growth. God hedged me and I had grown to like where He had me. I'd grown to trust Him with the fence line. I couldn't stay staring at it. Instead, I felt curious: *Why here? Why stuck inside? Why now?* Not angry but inquiring of Him—my Dad.

I hadn't always been curious. During the first years that produced limitations, I made friends with resentment, envy, and anger, the triad that often excludes curiosity.

To receive our limits as gifts—to even be able to untie our shoes, slide off our socks, and step our bare toes onto the squishy, absorbent earth where we stand—we must first notice our responses to them. We must first understand our history with our limits, how we've handled them.

At twenty and lonely, I dreamed about having someone to share my bathroom sink and my long late-night hours. At twenty-four and ministry-tired, I daydreamed about the next vacation, the next poolside day, baking mindlessly in the sun. At twenty-eight and surrounded by round-bellied friends, I daydreamed about bedrooms that held children, not guest amenities. And at thirty-four with four children, I daydreamed back to my earlier days, daydreams filled with real, old memories when I could read chapters, not pages, of books uninterrupted. I daydreamed about smooth counters without honey and peanut butter and empty laundry baskets.

No one ever told me this unexamined daydreaming could be a trap. It was as much a part of me as my right arm, put to everyday use without my noticing. Daydreaming was an unthinking part of my life, always accessible, never evaluated. It traveled with me into a friend's new kitchen, forming ideas of how to upgrade mine, and into a conflict with a child, reminding me what my life could be if this child's behavior would simply change.

Naturally, as I faced limitations, daydreaming accompanied my coping strategies. I saw myself as limited within an early marriage with a lot of conflict, and I dreamed about days when we weren't tied to a covenant or days when the conflict would miraculously lift and we could share sheets and secrets and warm feelings.

Unfettered thinking. Not captured but let loose. When I read Scripture verses such as Romans 12:2, where Paul says, "Do not be conformed to this world, but be transformed by the renewal of your mind, that by testing you may discern what is the will of God, what is good and acceptable and perfect" (ESV), I naturally thought of my outward actions being willed into submission. I ignored Paul's word about our *minds* being renewed, or if I did consider it, I thought most naturally about my jealous, angry, anxious thoughts—the obvious troublesome ones—not about my daydreams.

But when I examined a single day, it was full of daydreams, unthinking dreams that seemed harmless but, without thoughtfulness, opposed my mind to the place where my feet stood. It was a world of its own, but one that wasn't real, so it also wasn't one in which I invited God's input or wisdom. These daydreams aligned me with this world, doubting the fatherly hand of God, tossed like a wave of the sea driven by the wind (James 1:6). They were nearly undetectable: dreaming of when my daughter would be five, not two, and no longer in diapers; imagining a more leisurely life with another teenage driver and not so many hours of carpooling;

picturing when we might replace our carpet—surely a cleaner floor might mean a less clouded mind. Envisioning ways to optimize the tiny challenges in my life seemed harmless enough, except these ideas occupied space in a finite mind. They made me a hurdler, seeing the fence as something to overcome rather than exploring what it was intended to be. With many glances over the fence, I resented what it held inside.

My thoughts were unevaluated. Minutes could quickly become hours over days, then weeks, then years of those subtle inkling daydreams alluring me to figure out how to make them real. Not only did they breed discontent deep within the unnamed places in my soul, but they caused me to use muscles I wasn't intended to use to move me past where I stood.

I pushed a child past their age-appropriate limits to bring more ease to my life.

I escaped to the beach, hoping it would reset my perspective on my unvacated life.

I lived more online than in person because in-person felt too vulnerable and risky.

I walked too soon on a broken ankle and pushed my postpartum body into running shorts and a T-shirt before it was healed.

I missed my husband's heart as I manipulate my responses to his behavior to get him to change rather than grow.

I overlooked my child's special needs to make our life feel more normal.

There is a thin line between strategies for improvement and strategies that disrupt the life God has placed us in. Sometimes the vacation is necessary for a reset, and urging a child to step forward, not stay static, an act of love. Much on my list could have its rightful place.

Our posture in these moments should be an invitation rather

than a shortcut. "You know my thoughts even when I'm far away," says the psalmist (Ps. 139:2 NLT). God knows our daydreams, and we have the opportunity to invite Him to speak into them, to be with us inside of them bringing His understanding of motives and intents and longings.

Fourteen years ago, I suffered heatstroke in sight of the finish line of a community race I'd been training to win.

It was eighty degrees with high humidity, and I'd trained for months on seventy-degree mornings—unusually cool for summer. I had written on my hand my time goals for each mile—my splits, as they're called in the running world. My brain locked on to those times, and I achieved most of them until the last mile, when I began losing my mind. I learned later that it's common among those who suffer heatstrokes: they ignore the signs their body is giving them to stop. When the stroke occurs, the body has already offered up many signals, many cries for help, to pause, to slow, to drink water. Finally, when provided no relief, the body shuts down.

There was no space for me to hear the warnings, to pay attention to what my body was telling me. My mind was fixed on those splits, on the attempt to win.

We are embodied. Limited. Full of dreams and passions for abundance, and yet requiring seven to eight hours of sleep and sixty-four ounces of water daily to function well.

We have eternity in our hearts, and yet we can fracture an ankle, suffer a headache for days, scrape the skin right off a shin in one fall.

This story returned to me as I faced a year that held significant surprises and significant hurts. For a while, as I fielded those, I kept the pace. Daily dinner for nine, groceries delivered on time, texts replied to on the same day, others' expectations met. I was fixed on my splits, though unknowingly.

And then my body said uncle.

Month after month I found myself sick, each time with an explanation until there were no more. Friends came through town a day after they cleared the stomach bug, so of course I got it next. I prepped our family of nine for a cross-country trip and then we drove it. Of course, with disrupted schedules and little girls waking in the night in unfamiliar homes, I was bound to get sick. But after several months of recurring sickness and waning explanations, I realized I had been watching my splits. Still serving dinner around the table, still taking family trips, still bringing meals to friends in need, ignoring my own needs. The temperature rose, life got heavier, and still I drove myself.

So I stopped watching my splits and gave in to the tired. I paused the yeses to help friends and ordered takeout and went to bed early, even amid teenagers whose hearts open after 9:30 p.m. It was the best decision of my year.

Tired can be a gift, friends. But many of us are living like we're still in our twenties and like I ran in that race: we press through tired. We ignore it. We charge through the limit it imposes on us.

God encased us in flesh. He gave us wrinkles and gray hair and the need for sleep and sunshine and water and bathrooms. Is it too much to consider that He uses our bodies to reach us, telling us when to pause, to slow, or to sleep?

"Do you not know that your bodies are temples of the Holy Spirit, who is in you, whom you have received from God? You are not your own" (1 Cor. 6:19).

We all would agree God cares about this temple, this holding place for Him, but He also uses it to teach us, to reach us.

Is your steady midafternoon fatigue telling a story? Could it be God is using it to reach you, to reveal to you how you've ignored your limits?

So many of us run our Christian race like I ran that four-miler all those years ago: eyes on the splits, convinced that we know the goal, idealized against hearing and receiving God's gentle, persistent warnings to realign us toward His way.

We press on, but not in the way Paul intended when he said, "I press on toward the goal for the prize of the upward call of God in Christ Jesus" (Phil. 3:14 ESV). We press through, ignoring the way God made us to achieve a prize that, though we use language as if it's in the name of God, often just makes us feel better about ourselves.

Perhaps we've not seen or named this struggle with our limits. Maybe we've not noticed the way it drives us.

And then there are the times when we can't push through anymore and, rather than giving way to relief, stew in envy. We take slow drags of the poison of resentment and comparison.

R. C. Sproul said, "The minute we are envious and jealous of another, we have banished God from our minds."[1]

Harshly put, perhaps stark. But true?

Can my mind bow to the truth of how God operates within me and also serve the resentment that grows like mold around my thinking as I respond to my limitations?

Many of the six thousand thoughts that pass through my mind in a day go unexamined. A wistful thought that my friend with two

1. R. C. Sproul, *Romans: An Expositional Commentary* (2009; Sanford, FL: Reformation Trust, 2019), 53.

children has an easier life than mine spasms like an unexpected sneeze, then is forgotten almost as quickly. Before I pull out of my driveway, a flashy new car passes my family van, and I wish away this gift for a shinier one—all in a second. A friend's trip to Europe and another's wrinkleless face fill my thoughts—for ten seconds or twenty—and then I move ahead.

But do I?

Envy has morphed and changed with me over the years. As I've grown in the trust that comes when life breaks you and God carries you, envy has lost its steam. But I would be naive not to note that my six thousand thoughts sometimes include wishes for my neighbor's lawn, my friend's free spirit, or my Pilates instructor's posture.

"A heart at peace gives life to the body, but envy rots the bones" (Prov. 14:30). The New Living Translation says jealousy is "like cancer in the bones." It's an apt metaphor. Silent, undetected until it can't be any longer, threatening to steal our life.

There are dozens of other ways we relate to our limits. Some of us stealthily work around them, and others form a life of avoiding them. We groan with our mouths, and others, more self-controlled, close our mouths and let cynicism seep out of our pores.

But that heart at peace, the one that gives life to the body—is it possible to carry that?

Several days ago, I walked through my house as if watching unedited movie footage. Room to room, I scanned without editing. No picking up socks or train cars. No quick swooping up the piece of laundry lint in the hallway. I came, uncharacteristically, to observe and not to fix.

What a sight this would have been for my thirty-year-old self. Laundry heaped a foot above the top of the basket, the lid cock-eyed and merely ornamental now. My cozy rocker—the one we painstakingly selected years ago, delivered days before Virginia was born—now stained by nursing babies and chocolate-fingered toddlers and holding four bags of clothes to be shipped back to the store.

I stepped over the muddy droplets on my bathroom tile, rem-nants from coming home after a morning run and being met with a chorus of "Mom, could you . . ." and "Mom, I need . . ." I had clearly failed to notice that I'd brought the trail in with me, but I moved forward now, choosing to overlook it.

Virginia's latest paintings rested on my bathroom counter—the one with the 1990s ceramic sink from Lowe's that is short enough for five-year-olds to store their masterpieces on.

Two thoughts vied for my attention. One was an old friend I'd known since I'd begun to see the world as two-toned: me versus another. The other was fresher, not entirely new but not as familiar as the old friend had been.

The first wanted to scold me, to turn my eye into a microscope. It drew my attention to the spilled makeup on the bathroom sink under Virginia's paintings, and the worn carpet, ready, years ago, to be made new. It wanted to coach me into better habits, ones I knew I couldn't reach with seven kids, and to shame me as I con-sidered them.

The second gave a moment's lift to my heart. *She's different,* I thought, comparing myself with the thirty-year-old version of me. A full hamper meant a full life—so much life to be lived in the woods behind our home that the tykes couldn't stay clean of the mud in between meals. It meant teenage daughters trying on multiple out-fits and asking their mama's opinion. "Does this look too tight?

Too baggy?" Sure, the hamper held clean discards that would have annoyed me years ago and did occasionally now, but my girls crowd their mama's room for outfit changes.

The art was hers—my "tender one," as she calls herself. "Am I the best artist you've ever seen?" she asks without guile.

What a delight, what a gift to scan this room with wiser eyes and to feel full and satisfied. What a gift to know that my feet were standing right where they belonged, hardened muddy droplets and all. This season limits just how tidy my home can be without driving myself and my family crazy, and it's not like I enjoy the clutter or the disarray. But in that moment, I didn't manufacture a plastic gratitude over silent resentment about my limitations. Instead, I had a bold and honest look at the fence line with eyes that were being trained to see the beauty of what's inside of it, not outside.

What if this is freedom?

The question dropped into my mind, foreign. *She* never would have called this freedom, that twentysomething girl who had places to go and didn't yet know she might not be able to get there. This would have been her bondage, this mess of a life—not the elements of it but its limitations. The reminders lie everywhere of a constrained life, an "I just can't do that right now" existence. Not enough time for laundry or a brilliant display of a child's art or creative meal-planning. Not enough resources for a needed renovation.

But time, and God, and grieving and healing, and healing and grieving, have been making me into someone who knows that the boundaries also contain wild flowers and zinnias and hummingbirds and soft grass. And freedom.

It's reverse technology: growing young makes a person wise and old. Being pigtailed and held—unsure of what tomorrow holds but sure of this single moment, alert to it and subject to trust within it—is how a person grows. Ever so slowly we learn to exchange our narrative for His—that our home isn't here; our home is Him. This isn't sermon-learning. It takes a life sequestered inside the fence line to find home.

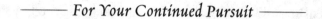

For Your Continued Pursuit

Psalm 16:6 | Psalm 139:2, 5–6 | Proverbs 14:30 | Ecclesiastes 3:11 | Matthew 6:24 | James 1:6–7 | James 3:16 | Romans 12:2 | 1 Corinthians 6:19 | 2 Corinthians 10:5 | Galatians 5:1 | Philippians 3:20–21 | Philippians 4:7

— 3 —

STORIED

Our Unexamined Perspective

> Telling a story is like reaching into a granary full of wheat and drawing out a handful. There is always more to tell than can be told.
> —WENDELL BERRY, *JAYBER CROW*

AT SEVEN-THIRTY ON THIS JANUARY MORNING, THE temperature read seventy degrees. On a rare trip to Maui—the "adventure of a lifetime," we called it—I carved a rhythm of morning runs along the ocean. Waveless, the sea looked like glass, but for occasional waterspouts; it was whale season. The sun silhouetted the mountains in the distance, yet I barely sweat. I could run for miles effortlessly in this warm winter air, mainly because the landscape distracted me from my rising heart rate. This was Candyland for an ocean lover.

I watched the people I passed along the path, curious whether anyone else was as wonderstruck as I was. Life felt peaceful here—vacation life is an escape for many—but was it also that hearts find rest when toes find the sand and eyes scan the sea line for whales? God settles us with His creation.

One family passed me as I ran, the path wide enough to fit two or three. An ambitious mom and dad running side by side, pushing their little one in a jogging stroller. The child, about three or four—the age of wonder—fixed her eyes on the device in her hand.

I don't judge this couple. This little girl with the matted hair could have been sleep deprived from a red-eye or homesick for her bed. Maybe she was sick, or the run was exceptionally long. All of us make parenting decisions hoping that we won't be evaluated by people who don't know the whole story. But in that flash, I saw myself in that child.

How often have I missed the wonder in front of me for the promise of something different elsewhere? I ran along mountains that rose out of the slick seascape, with the sun at an angle to reveal their beauty while whales breached in the distance. What a show. But for that little girl in the stroller (and so often for me), the screen in her hand offered more. She could travel to even more remote lands, see fancy impish creatures, and experience girlish delights. She could step outside of herself and into that screen and escape from paradise.

That child is you, and she's me, blind to the wonder of a cerulean ocean full of wild sea creatures in exchange for something that feels limitless but is actually full of restraints. Fooled. Duped, we constantly question whether God's boundaries are best. We think the picket fence is our nemesis, not where we find paradise.

The psalmist says, "You have fixed all the boundaries of the earth; you have made summer and winter" (Ps. 74:17 ESV). Anyone who lives in regions with long, cold winters spends the last couple of weeks of February and into March watching the weather for any sign of lifting—any bud, any shoot. We become ornithologists and weather casters, scientists of spring and expectant. We are limited by the hardened, snow-covered ground of December in a way that makes that first piercing sunshine of spring lift our hearts right out of our chests, just like the heat of August makes October's bonfires and s'mores all the more worth savoring. Apple orchards in summer are overlooked; in September, they're brilliant. Life within limits—the boundaries of seasons—mirrors the life within limits our Father grants. When we live where we are, we remember what we often forget: there is so much to see here, so much to consume.

We twenty-first-century humans have tried to live limitless within our limits; the cocktail of our flesh plus the culture and an uptick in technology invites us to climb into the worlds we see on our screens while forgetting our back yards and the life therein.

We look beyond the fence line all day long. Naturally, we want what we see. Nicer cars, trendier clothes, skinnier waistlines, and clean kitchens with a candle lit; children whose fingernails are not dirty, and mudrooms without mud. Though our bank accounts can't often support this lack of limits, we look for a way. Life-hacking is a value. If you bump into the fence and bruise your waist, it's not too high to climb. Shortcuts are celebrated. The life of slow growth and incremental movement is despised by our culture and then by us. Naturally, then, so are our limits.

But God not only endcapped our lives, determining the exact number of days, minutes, seconds that our lungs will breathe, but He gave us parameters within them. Our culture's narrative that we can get places faster, ameliorate our trials, and multitask toward better productivity opposes the life and daily assignments God gives that can't be optimized. As Eugene Peterson says in his book *Practice Resurrection,* "Maturity cannot be hurried, programmed, or tinkered with. There are no steroids available for growing up in

Christ more quickly. Impatient shortcuts land us in the dead ends of immaturity."[1]

And immature we are. I say that not to scold but to invite. We are young in understanding all it takes for a life to grow deep and long in God. We are adolescents desiring the "free" life and not yet aware of the house benefits we have been given.

But this gap in understanding didn't start with you and me. We haven't merely been handed a narrative we naively believed; we've been predisposed to desire that narrative. As different as our histories might be, we share the human craving to live outside the garden limits. Birthed into curiosity for what we were told not to touch, each one of us has a story that enflamed that curiosity and made us covet what lives outside our boundaries.

The story of how I got here is different from yours. There isn't a "one size fits all" grid for how and why we see limits the way we do. But sometimes it requires stepping into another's story to realize our own, to recognize that we, too, are storied.

My dad grew up with little. How little was little, I still don't know. He had shoes and clothes and an education. He went to college. His family celebrated the Fourth of July and gathered for Christmas. They lived in a home by the river and owned a typewriter. What I lack in hard facts is more than made up for by my experience of my dad, and I knew him as an overcomer.

I grew up hearing about my dad, who, on a whim, hiked the Grand Canyon with a Diet Coke in his hand. The story was true to

---

1. Eugene H. Peterson, *Practice Resurrection: A Conversation on Growing Up in Christ* (Grand Rapids: Eerdmans, 2013), 133.

what I knew of him: he was an adventure-seeker, willing to think outside the box, a dreamer. I grew up thinking I could do anything. I'm not sure whether he ever spoke those words to me, but it's what I received from him.

My daddy made a dreamer out of me. I took a few acting classes and performed secondary roles in several plays, and my heart was tied to Hollywood. I was inconsequential within my midwestern suburban life but dreamed big, like many children who hadn't yet bumped up against their boundaries.

I became a runner because of my dad. He saw me running across the neighbor's yard, as children do, and said to me, "You have a runner's form." *You can run* is what I received. So I did. I ran races, and his voice about my runner's gait was at my back like the wind for years. I wonder whether I heard it the day of my heatstroke, when I ran right through my body's limits.

You see, my dad grew up unseen by his dad, and he didn't have what he so freely gave me later on: a father who named the strengths he saw and coaxed me forward with dreams of what I could do. He had to find that within himself. So he overcame. He overcame scarcity, and coached tennis, and sold real estate, all while developing a program to keep high school dropouts in school. We vacationed every year as a family and lived comfortably. We weren't without like he was. He overcame and took us with him, my dad, to whom limits were intended to be challenged.

If we were merely evolving creatures, ever so slightly more advanced than those who went before us, this narrative of upward and onward growth might be how we pattern our lives. My dad's ceiling should be my floor. But in the way of God, growth isn't always upward and onward. All narratives find their proper place within His. And His pattern for growth is often slow and even sometimes circular. He refers to Himself as the God of Abraham, the God of

Isaac, and the God of Jacob—three men with intertwined stories and nuanced hearts. He is God to all of them, storied inside of their stories. All narratives find their proper place within His.

I inherited my dad's overcoming. His blood coursed through my veins when I ran that four-miler and when I set spiritual goals for myself—evangelism goals—in my early twenties that sought to exceed what had been done before me. I was Daddy's girl.

But his body stopped overcoming too early; my dad died young. Sheer will wasn't enough to defy limits. There was a different kind of overcoming he came to understand in the months before he died. I understood it in the years after I stood at his grave. Finally, he stopped trying so hard to be good and do life right, and became a son, again and for the first time, of God.

We are storied people. The fierce little girl who'd never taken a dance lesson in her life and yet stood on the spotlighted stage of a downtown theater and answered a hearty "Yes!" when the director asked her, "Can ya dance?" had a reason for her yes. And as with all the layers of life, some of that vim and vigor was part of how God made me, and some of the limit-defying drive was inherited from a man who learned that to survive, he had to overcome—until he couldn't overcome and Jesus met him.

We are a medley of our stories and His work around and through them. Your response to your limitations—how you view your fence line and how you respond to it—though at times might be similar to mine or to your neighbor's, is wrapped up in your story.

Charles Spurgeon said, "There never was a time in which we were unknown to God, and there will never be a moment in which we shall be beyond his observation."[2] He saw when you were deter-

---

2. Charles Spurgeon, *The Treasury of David: Classic Reflections on the Wisdom of the Psalms* (Peabody, MA: Hendrickson, 2014), 259.

mined to win the spelling bee in the third grade and when you vowed never again to let Susy Swanson beat you in the fifty-yard dash. He is acquainted with all of our ways (Ps. 139:3). And His knowing reveals the significance of being known within our stories. He sees what matters to us, and He understands our ways. He cares for what we care for.

I can't look at my response to my limits without being willing to invite Him to speak into what He already knows: my history with limitations and how my reactions to them were formed.

In less than twenty-four hours, three invitations came to us—ones that, years before, would have been easy yeses. The first was a text from a friend wanting to host a few couples for marriage refreshing, late-night conversation, and easy time together—sages and trusted friends from across the country. "Pick a date that would work for you" was essentially her ask. Except no date worked. With teenagers and diapers and our quarterly (and necessary) marriage getaway already scheduled, we couldn't add another thing. Not this year. The other couples had launched their children or had just one or two, not seven across life stages.

Then the following day, Nate was invited to go camping with a group of guys. Except it was only days before our family trip across the country, and he knew it would deprive him of the sleep he'd need to drive our family to the beach.

And in the middle of this, an offer to lead a course on a topic we both love and about which we're passionate. But when?

It felt like a tease. Not just one but three things we'd love, things I was sure would grow us, the good things of God. Fruit, but on the other side of the fence, the tree I couldn't reach. Or rather the tree I *could* reach if I stretched, and from which I knew I had been asked not to eat.

I have lived this moment dozens of times, revealing dozens of ways I have seen God and dozens of ways my history has informed my seeing more than His Word—this tug-of-war where we stand on the sidelines and wonder, watchful, who will win. Will my story and history and the inertia of generations before me win out, or will a perspective on God that sets me free align me?

I could feel teased, forever chasing a dream like a river rock skipping away from me, only to sink. The God on the other end of that teasing is the one I imagined in the back of my mind many times, taunting me with what He has that I don't, leaving me to assume that He must be good and I must not. Tempting me to lean into overcoming to prove I won't be led by the nose.

But there's a whisper at the end of those three invitations. It's quiet, not forceful. This whisper is a gentleman, ready when I want to hear and silent if I just can't be. The whisper sounds something like *I hold your lot* (Ps. 16:5). *I hold it all. You live it. I maintain it. It's mine to give and yours to walk out. Within these boundaries, there is life.*

These three invitations came fourteen years after the heatstroke. The whisper wasn't new, as it had been a decade and a half earlier. I didn't just have the history of being a child of my father, the overcomer, but I was starting to build a history of hearing His whisper in and through my story, making sense of it all and me within it. Trusting God as the narrator of our stories, even if it's a walk back through old scrapbooks and yearbooks, teaches us to slowly trust His voice, the whisper. Something felt secure in knowing I couldn't overcome but needed to succumb.

This growing pain—our no in the face of good and exciting invitations—was just like my son experiences growing pains: an ache in the night, at ease in the morning. It felt fresh and free to say these nos and then move forward with the unnegotiable yeses of our family and our marriage and the few things we could consistently do to sustain those. Perhaps this peace is the fruit of slowly moving toward seeing ourselves within the whole of our story.

Curt Thompson said in *Anatomy of the Soul,* "God will search the inner rooms of our hearts. That, however, does not guarantee that we will be present where he is looking and challenging. It is one thing for God to search. It is quite another for me to feel searched. It requires me to be present, which requires work."[3] Merely knowing the history of my dad and his dad is not the same as inviting God into my story and asking for His input and interpretation and tender voice over those scrapbook pages. He searched me in those days and now, but will I ask Him for what He found? Will I receive what He discovered as He went caving in my soul?

The little girl who inherited her father's overcoming spirit also inherited a sense of abandonment when she couldn't overcome—a loneliness inside her fence line, a fear that she might always be stuck with what was given to her, a resentment of her limitations. These things have needed God's gentle, calloused hands to smooth them through—to hold them, to knead them, not to despise them but to illuminate them.

In that story, the image of God as one who teases and taunts with the things we cannot have slowly evaporates. Who He is becomes more real than my history tells me. But I can't be re-informed if I don't invite Him into what initially informed me.

Jerry Sittser, a man who lost his mother, his wife, and his four-year-old daughter in one harrowing night, one harrowing car crash,

---

3. Curt Thompson, *Anatomy of the Soul: Surprising Connections between Neuroscience and Spiritual Practices That Can Transform Your Life and Relationships* (Carol Stream, IL: Tyndale Refresh, 2010), 176.

said, "Much of who I am is a product of the heritage given me at birth. My story is part of a much larger story that I did not choose. I was assigned a role for which I did not audition. Yet I have the power to choose how I will live out that story and play that role."[4]

We may not be able to choose our stories, but that does not mean we live without choices.

Years ago, a new acquaintance chatted with me about his time on the mission field. He told me about how his son had been traumatized by an experience they had in this impoverished nation, and how the terror that struck this young child's heart was enough to send them back to the States.

It had been years since his family had returned to the States, and his children were grown now, and as he described the impact of this event on his son, this gentleman said to me, "But the great thing is, now, you'd never know. You'd look at him and never know."

This statement hung in my mind. Our culture celebrates *you'd look at him and never know.*

While the depth of this statement (and likely even what this man meant) is a beautiful goal—oh, to be a people who so radiate the life of Jesus that the light and momentary "deaths" to our bodies are overshadowed—so many of us live only on the surface of it, hoping to hide our scars. The scars that make us who we are.

"For we who live are always being given over to death for Jesus' sake, so that the life of Jesus also may be manifested in our mortal flesh" (2 Cor. 4:11 ESV). There is a lot of death in a story that ever

---

4. Jerry Sittser, *A Grace Disguised: How the Soul Grows through Loss,* revised and expanded (Grand Rapids: Zondervan, 2021), 186.

so slowly is eking out His life—often tiny deaths, along the way, that each one of us experience. But to overcome before we pause to consider, to grieve where necessary, to heal, is not really overcoming, it's circumventing. The ways we respond to all sorts of things in our lives—one of them being our limitations—are informed by pasts we didn't grieve or consider, or from which we didn't heal. We form a lifestyle around compensating for little-girl and little-boy dreams never met, gaps in our histories, when the invitation of God is to let the old be made new.

We celebrate *you'd look at him and never know* when perhaps God intended His light to shine through the scars. And we live *you'd look at him and never know* in dozens, if not hundreds, of little ways.

You'd look at him and never know applies to the girl who worked tirelessly to win the Bible quizzes of her childhood, but really to win her mom's affection. Mom always hugged her when she won.

You'd look at him and never know might be the best basketball player in the city earning herself a college scholarship to play ball. What you don't see under the gymnasium lights is a girl who drove herself for hours every day in an attempt to find herself in a world where home was pure chaos.

You'd look at him and never know was perhaps the son of an alcoholic father whose attachment to him was spotty at best. He rose through the ranks of full-time ministry, preaching the gospel with fire but feeling dismissed when he wasn't on the stage.

You'd look at him and never know might be what they'd say about you or me, and we might stand a little taller when they do, hopeful our past might become just as invisible to us as it is to them. But then we bump up against the fence line—scan our horizon and see it—and our response seems disproportionate, or perhaps our efforts to hurdle it fail. Your sick child isn't getting better, despite all the treatments and all the research you have done about all the possible treatments. Your marriage isn't miraculously changing after you return from the marriage retreat. Your friendships aren't growing in this new town, even though you keep putting yourself in the right place to meet people and cultivate new relationships. Your babies don't sleep through the night or your teenagers fail to turn their work in on time. All your dreams about your career seem like they have a fence line, and you're frustrated inside it. And it's not like you're growing any younger.

When we bump up against that fence, *you'd look at him and never know* is challenged. What if God intends for you to look at him and *know*? To look and see scars that didn't merely disappear with time, to see fractures that don't heal properly when the pressure increases, to see a weakness that needs a God to hold it and move through it gently?

What we want to erase and move past and overcome, God often wants to walk through with us.

Sometimes, God mercifully prevents us from finding our paths. The star basketball player incurs an injury before her final college season. The Bible quiz queen comes in fourth place. The preacher falls prey to sin that gets exposed, and the child for which we pray relentlessly for healing remains sick.

We land ourselves at a dead end and pray in one direction: *God, get me out.* Some of us pray this for years, decades. It's all we know to do when we face a limit. But this wall could be a hedge. And our constant prayers to climb this wall, to win against what we deem is the enemy, could also be vaporous cries into the night when God invites us to see and live and understand another narrative.

While there are seasons for ceaseless intercession, some of us have grown one-dimensional, insistent even, in our conversation with God when we want something past the fence line. And that might be the moment when He's inviting us to see how He parents us. It's also an invitation to examine why we respond to His parenting as we do.

The beginning of that gentle conversation—that soft unveiling that God does when He invites us back into our stories, with His hand on our backs and His whispering assurances near—may be the end of our property lines. We stand with our toes on the line of where we cannot, no matter how hard we try, go, and He says, Come, let's talk about a different story—the story of you, and the story of Me, in and through you.

And one day, on the other side of being so limited, people might just look at you and know where you have journeyed and who He is because of it.

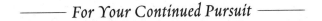

———— *For Your Continued Pursuit* ————

Genesis 2:15–17 | Exodus 3:15 | Job 14:5 | Psalm 74:17 | Psalm 139:1–7 | Hosea 2:6 | 2 Corinthians 4:7–12 | 2 Corinthians 5:17

4

A BRUSH WITH GOD

For whatever reason God chose to make man as he is—limited and suffering and subject to sorrows and death—He had the honesty and courage to take His own medicine. Whatever game He is playing with His creation, He has kept His own rules and played fair. He can exact nothing from man that He has not exacted from Himself.

—DOROTHY SAYERS, *THE GREATEST DRAMA EVER STAGED*

ONCE A YEAR, WE DRIVE THROUGH FIVE STATES OVER TWO days to spend a week at the beach with my family. Two passengers on an eighteen-plus-hour road trip might likely feel cramped and uncomfortable. We have nine. Nine suitcases, nine beach towels, snacks for nine, sleep comforts for nine—favorite pillows, favorite stuffed animals, favorite blankets (the down comforter I inherited from a college roommate twenty years ago is now Eden's and is leaving a trail of lost feathers behind it). When the sliding door of the oversized van-SUV we drive opens after we stop for fuel or restroom breaks, the wall of snacks and luggage lined against it topples onto the pavement—every time.

Before the trip, it takes me nearly a week to make lists and place orders, and then it takes two days to pack, all in preparation for the six we actually spend at the beach. The disproportionate amount of time we spend preparing for this trip compared with the time we spend with our feet in the sand and playing water games with cousins in the pool fades from our minds with our first glimpse of the ocean every year.

One year, however, we brought not only nine overly prepared packers but also a nasty virus. For days into a week and beyond, the glands in my neck swelled up like golf balls, and it took all my energy to swallow, much less talk. I spent most of the trip either in bed or half present and foggy. Without me, kids biked the rambling paths of this South Carolina beach town and built sandcastles. Nate lugged bags of beach towels down to the beach, and sandy bottoms back up to the beach house, day after day, as I struggled to sip water with a straw.

Conversations with nieces and nephews, late-night games, and catch-ups with my siblings didn't happen for me that year. The world went on without me, and I merely endured the beach trip for which I'd spent a week preparing and after which I'd spend days unpacking.

One of the nights of the trip, as I heard the laughter from the games downstairs—games for which my voice couldn't carry and my energy wouldn't sustain—I moped through getting myself to bed. This week felt like a microcosm of so much of my life: me, standing on the other side of the glass storefront, watching life happen inside, a life I couldn't reach. Had this week not come after many instances when I knew what I wanted but couldn't have, it might have been an isolated ache, but it was a bell on a long string of bells whose ringing made all the others chime.

As I padded around the bedroom that had become my cell, I toggled between praying, crying to God, and complaining, and then this question popped into my mind: *What if I meant for it to be this way?*

Hmm . . . I thought. *Surely this sickness is from the devil or the result of carelessness, not from God.*

I don't venture to guess whether the question was from Him, but the mere thought of God initiating my standing on the other side of the windowpane was a relief somehow. For the first time, I bumped up against my limitations and felt respite.

What if it *was* God? What if it wasn't the stress I'd been carrying in my body giving permission to a virus, or my not washing my hands thoroughly enough at rest stops? What if it wasn't another near miss of an opportunity, like the kind I'd felt so often to be a part of my story?

What if it was Him?

What once might have made me feel angry or overlooked gave me a pause in which I felt safe. My life was directed. I didn't need to orchestrate the details or secure the variables. I could exist and have life—as arranged by God—happen *to* me. Something sighed inside of me at this notion of being led, at the thought of my growing bouquet of stories creating a simple remembrance of this beauty and this truth: maybe I was made for this.

Something happened to my heart that week at the beach. Though I was missing out on in-depth conversations, heart-connections with my family, belly laughs, and the making of new memories, I felt like a child who woke up each morning wondering what the day would hold for her—less obligation, more receiving.

Hedged by the limits of my body, I was a child again at the beach. Palms open—a shell collector, an observer, a mere onlooker, a beneficiary. And something about this role set my little-girl heart racing as if riding a ten-speed bike for the first time. I could be *me*, receiving, unsure but led.

The fence line felt good at the beach that year. Real good. As if I was always meant to be that child, parented through limits and coming alive within them.

The biblical case for limitations—and a life that comes alive and lives within them—starts within skin.

"The Word became flesh and made His dwelling among us" (John 1:14). The God who architected sequoias and the tundra, jellyfish and peacocks—who knows the heart of a man and that causes the heart to beat in an embryo—put Himself inside of a body that burps and sweats and cries. The God who never sleeps became a man who got tired and thirsty. God limited Himself. He wore the boundaries of space and time and personhood.

We're invited to be "imitators of God, as beloved children" (Eph. 5:1 NASB), and His beloved child left the infinite to have a bedtime and body odor. His limitations, too, were purposed. "For this reason *he had to be made like them, fully human in every way*, in order that he might become a merciful and faithful high priest in service to God, and that he might make atonement for the sins of the people" (Heb. 2:17, emphasis added).

He had to, because in so doing he freed all who cowered through life (Heb. 2:15 Message). That's you and me.

His limitations mean that the haunting fear that keeps me up at night has a release valve. You don't have to bite your nails forever. The boogie man loses his wind for our little girls, and the office closing down doesn't mean a forever aimless wandering. Our worst fear crouching at the back door of our circumstances can't do what we always thought it would, because God limited Himself, first, so that He might not only be Lord over our limitations but also know intimately how it feels to have them.

God's choosing to limit Himself in His Son means that we receive a sympathy like none we have ever known, the kind of sympathy we don't imagine or for which we don't think to ask, but when it comes changes us—sympathy for our weaknesses, sympathy in the middle of the things we despise. It's not mere pity from the other end of the table. God gives us a knowing understanding through the Son who limited Himself so that we might be understood. Your barren womb or your pittance of a paycheck is understood not just in theory but in skin by the God who spun the stars into space and then fit Himself into skin that got acne and calves that cramped from walking long miles.

As John Donne said, "Others die martyrs, but Christ was born a martyr. He found Golgotha, where he was crucified, even in Bethlehem, where he was born; for to his tenderness then the straws were almost as sharp as the thorns after, and the manger as uneasy at first as the cross at last."[1] He is the Man who "in every respect" (Heb. 4:15 ESV) wore the weakness we live. His limits made Him one who sympathizes as He sees. The weakness we subtly despise, He knew. He knows—a byproduct of the incarnation, but no small one. I get a summer rash or fall into deep sleep in the middle of the afternoon after a long stretch of output. I weary of people and need a break. He knew these things, too. God knew because of the limits His Son took upon himself.

I resist my limits. I resent them. I work against them. I attempt to overcome them. And in Jesus' reaching for me, He leaned into

1. John Donne, "Sermon IV. Sermon Preached at S. Pauls on Christmas Day. 1626," Early English Books Online Text Creation Partnership, https://quod.lib.umich.edu/e /eebo2/A20637.0001.001/1:9.4?rgn=div2;view=fulltext.

them. He let them envelop Him. For a dark afternoon, they overcame Him. He died under them. But His leaning into limits meant a life that wasn't overcome, a life that won.

The sickness had lifted enough for me to have a nearly typical day on our last day at the beach. We set out our beach chairs as the tide went out, and the day and the beach stretched before us, larger and longer, for hours. We skipped afternoon rest time for the littlest ones and watched the sun leave red kisses on our towheaded children in trips between the shore and the tidal pool with buckets, attempting to capture the ocean and carry it home with us. Our big kids rode the waves, played paddleball, and walked the beach as if it were their last time there ever. We wrung the life out of our one full day as a family at the sea.

My heart was full, but less because I'd finally sunk my toes into the sand without thinking primarily about my golf-ball-sized glands. My heart was full because God gave me context for my limitations. I saw the blueprint: *this was meant to be.*

Brushes with God do that. They settle us. They give us perspective. They bring confusion into order and make sense of what feels senseless. Before this question dropped into my mind—*What if I meant for it to be this way?*—I'd been reading Scripture that had given it scaffolding.

Verses like James 1:2–4: "Count it all joy, my brothers, when you meet trials of various kinds, for you know that the testing of your faith produces steadfastness. And let steadfastness have its full effect, that you may be perfect and complete, lacking in nothing" (ESV).

And 1 Peter 4:12–13: "Beloved, do not be surprised at the

fiery trial when it comes upon you to test you, as though something strange were happening to you. But rejoice insofar as you share Christ's sufferings, that you may also rejoice and be glad when his glory is revealed" (ESV).

These were verses I'd written and rewritten in my journal in the weeks prior to our disrupted beach trip. They reminded me of things I'd forgotten in our optimized world: we're bound for scuffles in life, and they should not surprise us, because they are purposed. God had been building a framework for struggles as small as swollen glands on the beach trip and for others much bigger through which we'd been walking. But that night, in the single thought that gave me pause on the heels of my cry-praying to God, something shifted.

His Spirit counseled me.

These brushes with God change us.

When I was fifteen and said yes to Jesus, everything felt new. I saw the Creator and His pursuit of me in verses I'd read for the first time and heard Him in lines of old worship songs, which were new to me. My eyes looked for answered prayers. I leaned into expectancy. I shared stories with other new believers as if we'd all just discovered a hidden city right underneath us. I noticed all the details.

For a while after that period I looked back and considered myself naive. I didn't know pain or life-callouses then. I was wide eyed and maybe a little foolish. Underexperienced.

But He has a gentle way of growing us.

As it was with Eve.

In their newness, Adam and Eve were naked and "they felt no shame" (Gen. 2:25). Unboundaried.

But He put Eve in a garden with a tree she could not eat from.

Limits are one of the best ways He captures our attention, after all. That tree was a "delight to the eyes" (Gen. 3:6 ESV) for Eve: what she could not have allured her. It bedazzled her.

Was this just the fall of man or was it also God's ways in calling to our attention our craving for what we cannot have and then bringing that craving into the safety of trust?

If we don't name limits, we live captive to them, our attention continually averted from how He wants to meet us within the boundaried life to what we just can't have. But it's so subtle. A closer look at our daily thoughts reveals we wish we had an ever-so-slightly nicer car, cleaner home, better-paying job, more vacation time, better-behaved kids, thinner waistline, healthier constitution, happier marriage, just a wee bit more power or voice in our church or our small group. It might be ugly, but that closer look allows us to recognize and name our challenges, and that is the first step toward freedom.

The carpet on my second floor is fraying between the hallway and the doorframe to my daughters' room. I think about that half-inch fray and its splayed pieces at least once a day, wishing for an upgrade.

What I don't think about is that only one thing at a time can capture my attention. If unnamed—this competition within my head—I default to looking at the panorama beyond the fence.

But He doesn't settle for my default.

In our home with seven kids, there is a subtle vying for attention, as I'm sure is the case in any large family. The younger ones have the gift of their voices combined with a lack of inhibitions—louder, louder, louder still above the noise, just to be heard. In the midst of a weekend with houseguests who had children of all ages except hers, one of mine made her voice known. I saw the pain of her feeling on the outside and overlooked in a half-dozen ways, but my attempts to reach her felt unsuccessful. Mothers unable to meet their babies' needs are some of the squirliest individuals. We were made to soothe, and the times when we can't are unnerving.

I was so unnerved I barely prayed, so frayed I was hardly feeling.

A week after our guests were in town and my child was unraveling, I had been out for a few hours and pulled in at home in the evening to my son announcing that we had a new pet bunny. My unraveling child had been asking for a bunny relentlessly for weeks, and though I may have said an occasional maybe to assuage her, I knew our answer was no. Months earlier, I surprised Nate with a dog for his birthday. As a non-animal lover, I'd filled my quota for life on this side of eternity, by my measurements. So no hamsters, no bunnies, no cats.

However, my little one, persistent in having her voice heard above the noise, was relentless in pursuing the dream of a bunny. But even her ask made my mama-heart wince. Some nos are easily considered and hard to deliver. I just hurt for this kid.

So the announcement about the new pet bunny startled me. The big kids who were still awake led me to the front bushes, under which were four furless little animals that looked more like mice than bunnies. We shined our flashlights in the dark under the boxwoods to study them before searching the internet to be sure we had bunnies. We did.

My little girl had gone to bed an hour earlier, but she woke the next morning to the surprise under the bushes—four times as many bunnies as what she'd asked for.

Her answered prayers turned out to be a gift for me as well.

Her unraveling had stirred up all these latent thoughts in me: *Will all this noise in this jam-packed house ever produce thoughtful, intentional human beings, or will we have only an everyday war for attention?* Her tears reminded me of all we could not be as a family. They revealed my rarely named but often lived daydreams: a home where each child got their fill of Mom and Dad. A house where children didn't feel the need to fight for attention, each child feeling seen, known, and understood.

And I felt solely responsible for responding to those questions and desires for my family. I would never say that I was, but I lived as if I were. So her request for bunnies and God's response to the desire in her heart, outside of any of my efforts, was a gift to me as much as it was to her.

She ached, but I'm sure I hurt harder over the limitations of having seven bodies and hearts sharing one home. I ached for her times seven.

You see, my eye was on the fence line. I gave many minutes of my day to thinking about what I couldn't be for my kids because there were so many of them, what they wouldn't have in the crowd that was us, where we lacked in quality because we didn't lack in quantity.

But there was another story: God's reach for her, the one who hadn't been seen, who'd been overlooked.

Her voice wasn't loud enough in the mess of teenagers sitting on our countertops, interrupting each other, and pizza boxes strewn across our kitchen, but He heard her whisper-prayer. That weekend, alone, she didn't have a playmate and got lost in the shuffle of big kids talking about things she couldn't understand and in the churning in the kitchen as parents sought to feed the masses, but He gave her one—the one she wanted—days later.

The bunnies were for me, too, watching my vulnerable child be seen by God within the limitations of our family. That night on my knees in the mulch, crawling under the boxwood limbs to count bunnies and take pictures and marvel, I had a lump in my throat. *He met her.*

But really, He met me.

Two stories in this crowded house: a little girl whose voice doesn't carry, fenced out from what she wanted, and her mom, aching over what large-family life means for tenderhearted people. And God reached in.

The whirling life affords little opportunity to see this inreach, so we must look for it.

We must name the competition for our attention and our affection: will it be like it was for Eve, "the delight to the eyes," or will it be what satiates the soul, this God who reaches within the boundary lines to meet our little-girl and little-boy hearts with wonder and delight, even when we can't have what we want? Especially when we can't have what we want.

In Matthew 16:25–26 Jesus offers an ominous remark: "For whoever would save his life will lose it, but whoever loses his life for my sake will find it. For what will it profit a man if he gains the whole world and forfeits his soul? Or what shall a man give in return for his soul?" (ESV).

I felt proud to memorize this when I was seventeen and full of youthful imagination about how and when I might lose this life for Jesus. Decades later, I feel both sobered and hopeful as I reread this passage. I've chased the life I promised I'd lose when I was too young to understand all the losing I'd face, and I finally think I maybe, kind of, sort of don't want to keep chasing. Whether I'm immature or too honest or too tired of idealism, I can't say with honesty that I'm done chasing, but I can say that I'm starting to find there is life in the losing. And maybe more life in the losing than in the gaining of the whole world outside the fence line.

Maybe the brushes with God become cumulatively better, better for my waking and my sleeping and my staying present and my passion for pursuing God and my marriage and my friendships and my vibrancy of heart than if I could create them myself out of my daydreams.

I think Jesus is that good, that worthy of our wild and wide-eyed affection.

For Your Continued Pursuit

Genesis 2:25 | Genesis 3:6 | Psalm 36:7–9 | Jeremiah 31:14 | Matthew 8:23–24 | Matthew 16:25 | John 1:14 | John 4:6 | John 14:26–28 | John 19:28 | Ephesians 5:1 | Hebrews 2:15 | Hebrews 2:17 | Hebrews 4:15 | James 1:2–4 | 1 Peter 4:12–13

Part 2

SURRENDER

Dying to My Story and Receiving His

THE CYCLE REPEATS ITSELF WITH EVERY TURN AROUND the sun. Summer, fall, winter, and springtime, the predictable patterns of a world so unpredictable.

God gifts us with scaffolding, despite the fact that we wake today not knowing whether we will wake again tomorrow.

In the vast mystery of God, He did give us a Friday when the tree bore deep into the skin of His shoulders, a Saturday when we imagine the earth to have fallen silent and clouded, and a Sunday when new life emerged from what was lost. In the following chapters we'll explore the potential cyclical nature of our lives—this death, unto a mournful Saturday, but with the hope of a resurrection of what was lost and a heart landscape that, perhaps, looks quite new and different.

5

THE MYTH OF
DREAMING WITH GOD

Very truly I tell you, unless a kernel of wheat falls to
the ground and dies, it remains only a single seed. But
if it dies, it produces many seeds.

—JOHN 12:24

I WORE IDEALISM AS A BADGE OF HONOR WHEN I WAS
younger. It meant that I had my eyes set elsewhere, that I had
vision for more than my four walls or my small life could hold.
My generation took the "great cloud of witnesses" seriously.
Imaginary applause filled our minds as we envisioned celebration of our excellence by our peers and leaders. We were
dreamers, visionaries, uncomfortable with mediocrity. Jesus
was excellent, and so we should be excellent.

My idealism looked much like the dining hall did the summer
when I was seventeen and I worked at a camp in the Adirondacks.
From seven in the morning until after dark, I waited tables, serving camp food to teenagers, many of whom would meet Jesus that

week, just as I had a year before. Our waitstaff were other teenage dreamers like me. Earnest, excellent ones, focused on the excellence of Christ, on display through things we could make excellent. We cared about our participation in His beautiful work. This was our contribution to the salvation of souls.

Many of us new believers and charged with excellence, we'd set the table for breakfast and then stand at the end of count-less rows of ten-tops, ensuring that every napkin fell directly in line with the napkins on the table after it and the one after that. We placed a fork precisely in the center of each napkin, and we stood at either end of the dining hall, measuring with our eyes, to ensure that each of the plates was in a perfect line from one table to the next. We made a museum of that dining hall, wiping finger-prints off of glasses minutes before groggy, unobservant teenagers stumbled into their seats with bedheads and bad breath, some still in their pajamas.

I'm grateful I learned excellence that summer. The dining hall was a neutral ground for having fun with ideals. And the idealist in me, intertwined with His heart, came on display in the dining hall. As I look back, I imagine God enjoyed the ways in which I found a type of holy ground in place settings. But perhaps placing the knives all the same number of inches from the edge of the table (because, if we had extra time, we did measure them) had less of a connection to the number of souls saved, as I rationalized it would, than it did to the confusion in my heart. Not just at seventeen but at twenty-three and thirty-two, I wanted my life, like the place settings in that dining hall, to be exacting and filled with excellence. Row after row of neatly folded napkins and polished forks: a symphony of order. A dream.

It all seemed so right. Who wouldn't extrapolate that the God who gave us the equinoxes and ant hills and gravity desire this sort of excellent order from His people?

This was one fairly easy-to-identify way my ideals filled my head.

The problem, of course, is that I didn't dream only about place settings. Well manicured schedules and Bible reading plans and parenting strategies all served my hunger to live in a fantasy, this ideal for life in God. They were not big dreams but tiny daily dreams with an outsized potency to wreak havoc.

The ideals I formulated over years for life in God and marriage and motherhood and vacations and even my wardrobe came from something so beautiful: they came from Him. God's way is perfect (Ps. 18:30 NKJV). He painted rainbows and formed the Alps and gave us bald eagles. We have seasons and hours and minutes that all repeat. Only God could imagine these. God is the ideal, and we want what He made us for.

But we get shifty, wanting something quicker and slicker than it comes or in a way He didn't intend. We reach lower than the sky for what we can touch and create and spin that feels and looks like Him. My ideals had more power than I realized before I named them. Before I noticed them.

The year I turned forty-one, I found their name.

A month or so into that year, I packed away the last of our baby gear—the giant Legos and soft teething blocks I stepped on in the night, the clunky diaper bag, and the infant car seat stained with avocado and browning banana and other sticky mysteries. I felt a bit of freedom as I loaded the chaos into extra-large black trash bags to give away to someone who wasn't sleeping at night and barely had time to shower.

Simultaneously, our oldest children faced new hiccups to what should have been a typical teenage existence but wasn't because of their history. I turned in burp cloths for a different kind of limitation in this season.

Life felt pressed, but at least the end of diapers was in sight. Reprieve of any sort feels glorious when life cramps.

One Wednesday night, I lay in bed next to Nate, awake, with tears, like rain on a windshield, finding their way down the sides of my face onto my pillow. "There just isn't enough of me for their needs," I choked. I hated saying out loud what I'd been working countless days to prove false. All the systems I had for triage of my children's needs were frequently being challenged: a toddler crying, a five-year-old's curiosity irritating a sibling doing their homework, a teenager stuck in angst, all shared in the same minute. Even my best impulses regarding which I needed to respond to first were fried. I woke up tired and fell into bed tired. I was constantly feeling never enough, living with my self-graded test score: C minus.

We came to no resolution that night. He prayed for me, and I cried harder. I fell into sleep and woke up realizing the gap between what I dreamed about for this season and the reality of living with both two-year-old and teenage emotions. Just like I had the day before. Just like I would the next day.

Finally on Friday morning, I took a "just to rule it out" pregnancy test. Blurry-eyed and carrying in my mouth that morning taste of the dissonance between dreams and reality, I leaned into my fifteen-year-old Hallmark theology: surely God wouldn't give me more than I could handle.

Except I was wrong.

There wasn't enough of me for the needs of six children, and now God was giving me a seventh.

We'd walked through infertility for more than a decade. Back then, I used to joke that I wished Costco sold pregnancy tests, though the joke tasted bitter as I said it. Ever hopeful, we nearly made them a line item in our budget. I dreamed for years about two thin lines, only ever knowing just one. I attended baby showers that left me crumbling. I should have had a frequent-visitor card for the fourth floor of Martha Jefferson Hospital—my home away from home as I visited friends who were having first, second, and third babies. Then, after twelve years on that road, God opened my womb. Again, and again, and again. And now, I'd learned this morning, *again*. (All of my pregnancies were called geriatric pregnancies.)

A glance at my story would have you scratching your head: she wanted this for years; now look at her ungratefulness. But many of us, unknowingly, do the dance of wanting not too much and not too little; either end of the spectrum feels like we're limited by desire. This was me.

In the following weeks, this mom, who wasn't enough for her six before her body formed another, found new limits. Forty-one and pregnant, my body craved an 8:30 p.m. bedtime and at least an hour's nap in the afternoon. I was tired before carrying this baby, but now a new kind of exhaustion left me no energy to press through. My teenagers had late-night events I couldn't attend because my body couldn't make it past sundown. Their hearts, so prone to unfurling after 9:00 p.m., found a listening ear in Dad while Mom snored down the hall.

Family dinners became utilitarian. I fed my people what I could cook with little time and energy. We stopped hosting monthly meetings and dinners with friends. I forgot my love for hospitality as I crawled through each day. My two-year-old became a daddy's girl that year, the year he woke her up in the mornings and got her dressed and end-capped her day by putting her into her pajamas and tucking her into bed. I hung back in the shadows, growing this baby and wanting to name the deeper ache of my heart that I somehow knew needed a name to heal.

You see, a few months into the pregnancy, with reluctance, I realized that I wasn't just growing this baby but also this baby was growing me. After the shock fog faded, I saw through what felt like an impossible call to raise seven humans that God might have something for me in this pressure.

Six wasn't the number that would drown me. Even the needs of my older kids, related to their childhood traumas, weren't the source of my overwhelm. I saw a more significant source of discord on my insides: the distance between my dreams for this season and my reality. I resented the fence line. Again.

The Webster's 1828 dictionary defines idealism as "the system or theory that makes every thing to consist in ideas, and denies the existence of material bodies."[1]

I lived celebrating ideas and ignorant of the cost described in the second part of this definition: that to keep fueling the ideas, the ideals, I had to deny what was real in front of me.

Every day there were choices: would I choose to hear this child's pain or redirect them to the place I wanted them to be? Would I step over tiny Legos and Matchbox cars to reach the child who needed to be scooped into my arms, or would I stop the world to recreate order in a disheveled family room? Would I talk to God from the place of lack, or would I end the day grumpy over where my home, my family, and my children's hearts were not, subconsciously making plans to get them where I needed them? Most of the time, I chose the latter.

Those late-night tears into my pillow had less to do with what was tangibly in my home (though those things *were* hard) and more to do with the everyday chasm between the ideas in my head and the bodies and hearts I was raising. I woke to a gap, spent my days

---

1. Noah Webster, *An American Dictionary of the English Language* (West Valley City, UT: Walking Lion Press, 1828), 368.

trying to bridge it, and went to bed disappointed that I'd failed. Seven hours of sleep and a little quiet with the Lord before the babes woke gave me more time to dream, to foster my ideals, and to fuel false hope that my ideals would come true on this day, even though they hadn't yesterday.

For most of my life, I admired people who were driven by their ideals, whose feet didn't always touch the ground. I took notes on them, followed their ways. I pursued teaching from leaders who had their heads, dreams, and visions in another world. It always felt better that way. (And wasn't that godly? Wasn't that living by faith, not by sight?)

But after I finally named a source of much of my discontent (my idealism), I began to separate the sweet inception of idealism—the little-girl dreamer who was made for another world—from my clinging to ideals more than to Him. Ideals felt like an easy cover for the discontent that was bigger than I knew how to name. And I began to see the cost in my children's lives. They needed a mom for where they were, not for where I wanted them to be. They needed to be held, not to be called higher and away from growing through their moment. Their lives needed a representation of Jesus, who came to hold hands, wash feet, and weep with His people.

You see, the pursuit of idealism makes us want to skip steps. To cheat, even. And in so doing, it's our hearts that get cheated as idealism diffuses hope.

I lived with a low-grade dissatisfaction with my days, constantly comparing my circumstances with my mostly unspoken ideals. I thought I was sowing into a dream of God's heart, but really I was trying to avoid feeling the pain of what wasn't. I would see a child struggling compared with their peers—compared with my friend's kids—and instead of noticing how that comparison brought a heaviness to my heart, I'd want to move that child toward change. I'd even pray that child toward change. (Sometimes idealism is revealed in the dogged drive of our intercession.) On a surface level, I'd dream about an ordered home, and when the inevitable disorder of many children made that dream challenging, I'd stay up later or work to hone more systems. I'd hound children to clean up more thoroughly. I spent immeasurable effort attempting to bridge the gap between my ideals and the messy gifts that stood right in front of me.

Some of you know this pain, working in a job that doesn't deploy you as you'd hoped, living in a city that isn't providing community, attending a church where you haven't found your group, residing in a family where you feel alone, raising a child who does not want to live your dream for them, enduring a marriage that is hanging on by a covenant, and on and on.

What isn't rarely gets named, yet its power in and throughout our lives is unparalleled. Our cynicism, our sarcasm and biting remarks, our jealousy, our inability to celebrate another, our sleepless nights, our dry times in His Word, our countless arguments: could they all be tied to how we handle it when our lives are not the ideas we'd invested in? Could they be connected to how we look at life within the fence line when what's on the other side is within sight but wholly out of reach?

But if it were named—if we called it idealism and we noticed the parts of our lives that fall short—might there be another road for that little dreamer?

Idealism can become an intoxicating way of avoiding the pain of what's real, right in front of us.

The temptation when we're faced with a life that isn't matching our ideals is to lose the ability to live in what's real and, instead, to imbibe discontentment. Of course, we dream about the family Christmas, gathered around the fire with eggnog and laughter, rather than the reality that every year, three hours in, the distant stance and sarcastic language begin. (Many of us continue to dream this dream starting on December 26, despite the evidence against it that we just lived—again—December 24 and 25.)

We are master pain avoiders, and idealism, cloaked in spiritual language, can become a sophisticated tool for those who'd rather not face the pain of what's in front of them. Negative emotions have little place in many expressions of our walk with God.

Eugene Peterson writes, "It is easy to be honest before God with our hallelujahs; it is somewhat more difficult to be honest with our hurts; it is nearly impossible to be honest before God in the dark emotions of our hate. So we commonly suppress our negative emotions."[2] The path of "it's all good" and "God's got this"—the dismissive phrases we say hoping they will assuage the pain—is easier.

But the Psalms are full of negative emotions and tell the stories of the ones who emote them and the God they find in the midst of them.

> "Out of the depths I cry to you, O LORD!" (Ps. 130:1 ESV).
> "My soul is in deep anguish. How long, LORD, how long?" (Ps. 6:3).
> "All my longings lie open before you, Lord; my sighing is not hidden from you. My heart pounds, my strength fails me; even the light has gone from my eyes. My friends and companions avoid me because of my wounds; my neighbors stay far away" (Ps. 38:9–11).

---

2. Eugene Peterson, *Answering God: The Psalms as Tools for Prayer* (San Francisco: HarperOne, 1989), 100.

"Why, Lord, do you stand far off? Why do you hide yourself
in times of trouble?" (Ps. 10:1).

Even Jesus used these words from Psalm 22:1: "My God, my
God, why have you forsaken me?"

In times of turmoil, believers explain away their emotions by
quoting portions of Scripture that say things like "do not be afraid,"
and I wonder whether it's not our theology but our discomfort that
prevents us from naming the emotions deep in our hearts that scare
us. If we see the whole of Scripture, even Jesus' words and emotions,
it's clear that God is not afraid of what we often squelch to live "a
more Christian response."

Many of us have spent so many years establishing patterns
of avoiding emotions that there is no explanation anymore—no
reasoning, just impulse. It feels bad, so avoid it. As Martyn Lloyd-
Jones said, "The average person . . . bases his whole idea of a God
of love solely upon his own thoughts."[3] We form deeper under-
standings of God that come not from His Word but from our
proclivities.

As you peer into the idealism I held not only during the months
I carried our baby Charlotte inside but also more subtly in other
areas of my life, do you see your own—instances when you reach for
what isn't, over and over again, and call it "dreaming with God" or
visionary living or holding out a hopeful perspective, at the expense
of bringing to God the pain of unmet ideals?

---

3. Martyn Lloyd-Jones, *Life in Christ: Studies in 1 John* (Wheaton, IL: Crossway,
2002), 432.

Unchecked idealism enables me to keep the Word at a distance from my heart, from the seat of my emotions, merely responding with my head and calling it hope and optimism. Idealism keeps me from naming the valley of the shadow of death, even though my legs tire from stumbling through it. While that avoidance can be peaceful for a while, it's a false peace. When I can name what's hard, I have a place to invite God. I can reach for His peace, rather than relying on my fabrication of it. When we fall for the mirage of idealism, rather than letting the Word reach, reveal, and meet what is actually inside of us, we are skipping steps.

A dear friend sent a message to a few of us, begging for prayer but really wanting to be seen in her pain. Her family was in an unexpected transition that proved to hold great grief, fear, and even shame for each of them. *What's next?* felt ominous, not inviting. I thought as I read and considered where she was that the younger version of me would have sent her Scripture to cast off that fear, to declare that she should be confident in the Lord. And while those verses are significant and necessary for moving forward, the moment required instead a stillness of grief for her and her friends—us—whom she'd invited to see her. (And it also needed me to trust that if I didn't send just the right verse or the right advice, God was still leading my friend.)

The walk through the valley of the shadow of death enables us to find a shepherd, to study the staff, to feel the protection of the rod. Without that walk—where our legs, which feel as heavy as trunks of aged trees, move and our feet feel the rocky divots of the valley; where our eyes experience the darkness as the mountains around us shadow us from the sun during the day and block the moon by night—the knowledge of God as shepherd, the significance of His staff, and the power of His rod are merely words.

"Behold, I stand at the door and knock. If anyone hears my

voice and opens the door, I will come in to him and eat with him, and he with me" (Rev. 3:20 ESV). Sometimes I picture God standing at the door of the emotions I have locked, asking for a meal, here. Right here.

Idealism left me with my head in ideas and my knees far from the floorboards where I might have kneeled out of sheer exhaustion and said, "Help, God." Idealism left me trusting the story, the vision, the dream, and trustless toward God. But it all felt so good and so right—my dreams for our family and my motherhood and my children's healing and wholeness. My eyes danced around what was on the other side of the fence.

Could the danger of unfettered idealism—of the dreamer on her bike given full range of the city before she's able to take the training wheels off—be in pursuing a dream that keeps God at a distance, a dream that somehow I'm calling His?

The months I carried that surprise baby in my belly and slept ten hours a night and served my family take-out on paper plates and missed a lot of voice recitals, lacrosse games, and theater performances were months when I found a name for what was keeping me from a deeper connection with God.

It felt like the valley, but until I named it as such and gave myself permission to lament, just like Jesus did on the cross, I was stuck. Morning after morning I plodded my way through Psalm 23. I needed a map, and this psalm was it. I didn't move on to the next verse until I traveled the current verse in my heart.

Psalm 23:1 reads, "The LORD is my shepherd; I shall not want" (ESV). I broke what I thought was a holy silence but was just a wall I'd erected between God and me, and I told God that I didn't feel shepherded. I felt alone and overlooked. It felt as if He were drowning me in my circumstances—me, with a great desire to meet my children's needs and now having too many needs to meet.

I chose honesty over Christianese. I practiced what I learned from the psalmists while holding His Word in my lap and saying it back to my heart. This was not a means of declaring as a cheerleader from the sidelines what was true to my heart, as if my heart would somehow, engaging in call-and-response, start to believe the words. His Word was a tether as I did the awkward naming of emotions that needn't have been awkward, because God made them, but was awkward because I was unfamiliar with them.

Slowly, over weeks and into months, I walked through the valley as I walked through Psalm 23, and somewhere in there, I learned, in my own life, how and why David could move from the third person in verses 1–3 to the first person in verse 4, where he says, "You are with me." It's no longer He—He is my shepherd, He leads me, He restores—but it's as if David looks God squarely in the eye and says "You."

And I did as well. *Finally.*

The layers of striving and strategizing and optimizing may have protected me from my emotions, but they also kept me from seeing a little girl who just needed to be held in her valley. Without idealism, it was me—the little-girl dreamer—and God. God and me. No longer me plus God plus my dreams and ideals. Just me, the whimsical dreamer, tired and needing a new way, and God. I looked at Him and said "You." He was no longer in the distance but near to my pain and what was real. My dreaming didn't threaten him; He made me that way.

But it was time to die to those dreams so I could find the God who made me a dreamer.

It's scary to let go of something as close to you as your skin.

Clinging to idealism helped me cope through the years when my dad was sick. Idealism drove my years in ministry. In full-time ministry, when the teenagers we were ministering to weren't saying yes to Jesus or following through with their faith, I kept dreaming of one day when they would. Round after round of the next big idea, the next big ministry plan or endeavor or sense from the Lord, kept me from the pain of what wasn't right now. Idealism was even a crutch in my infertility, helping me create visions and dreams to look forward to when I wanted to avoid the ache of my empty womb. Idealism whispered in my ear when we brought children across an ocean and into our home, when deep inside I felt terribly ill equipped to travel a distance that was measured not only in miles.

Without idealism, I was raw. Exposed. But I could finally sigh into a surrender of sorts: *What if His story is the one I've needed all along? I've contrived the best story in my mind, but to receive His, I must let go of mine.*

The death of idealism, which is inevitably slow, means an exchange of my dreams for His. "Very truly I tell you, unless a kernel of wheat falls to the ground and dies, it remains only a single seed. But if it dies, it produces many seeds" (John 12:24). An exchange of my leadership and initiative for His. Of my hopes, which fold under pressure, for His, which last.

And sometimes those dreams, that slow exchange, start small. Smaller than small. Smaller than we think. We put ourselves within His boundaries, which aren't supersized compared with our ideals but are safe.

Our unchecked human understanding tells us that bigger is better, but God often grows us small, slow, and undetectable. Embracing the limits He allows often feels far more restrictive than we imagine Him to be, but our growth is dependent on the exchange of our thoughts for His.

Dietrich Bonhoeffer, the man of the idyllic childhood and the grand plans for overturning the Third Reich, said this: "Things must go, not according to your understanding, but above your understanding. Submerge yourself in lack of understanding, and I will give you my understanding. Lack of understanding is real understanding; not knowing where you are going is really knowing where you are going."[4] When I humbly not only admit but live that my knowledge of a situation is, at best, grossly lacking full context and understanding, that is perhaps when I begin to live within my God-given story and not just wrestle with it.

A heart at peace is evidence of a heart that trusts.

Several years after our beloved, surprise baby Charlotte was born and we'd once again packed away our baby detritus, Nate and I stepped into more leadership roles in our everyday lives. As happens when seasons change and babies are done cutting teeth and middle-of-the-night feedings are no longer, we began to look beyond the nursery and the front porch. We had a bit more time.

Nate was invited to take a leadership role in our small house church. In the pioneering stage—one of Nate's favorite stages—it just made sense that he would lead. After many tired years, this was a welcome invitation. We prayed, and he said a wholehearted "yes, of course."

But just shy of a month later, I wondered: Was this indeed an *of course*? We certainly were less tired than when I was forty-two and birthing a child. Less tired than when we first navigated teenage

---

4. Dietrich Bonhoeffer, "Bearing Suffering," in *Be Still My Soul: Embracing God's Purpose and Provision in Suffering*, ed. Nancy Guthrie (Wheaton, IL: Crossway, 2010), 66.

years interlaced with childhood trauma. Less tired than when I had three children under six, plus four more to boot. Our instincts told us that we were ready to move on, pick up the pace, and take on more.

But in the quiet of the morning and in the recesses of our minds we both felt unsettled by this yes. In front of us was a bit more time and behind us was a lot more experience in the valley, which tends to be one of the best teachers on leadership, but the question became, "Is what's 'natural' God's intent for us?"

Some days of asking for counsel and prayer revealed this *yes, of course* needed instead to be a *no, not yet*, and we faced the awkwardness of saying no to what was once a yes, of breaking the ideal. "I made a mistake and committed before I realized I couldn't," Nate shared with the church.

In the weeks that followed, we sat in the small, the not yet, on the sidelines. And though the inertia would tell us this was a setback, something deep inside resonated with this step toward small. This was a step of surrender to His time and His ways. This was a reminder that we will always be the kids of God, our leader. And that He often gives us limits to grow us.

God's invitation dismantled my long-held ideas about what this stage of life would be. But the rest that came for our tired frames, which had grown a greater tolerance for tired than we had realized until we slowed down, felt like the gift of a good parent who serves you chicken soup in bed on a day when you could push through and says, "Not yet. Just another day to rest in bed."

The limitations God gives us can feel punitive and disruptive, out of time and deaf to our desires and dreams. Or they can feel light and caring, needed and deeply refreshing.

He knows best. Even when He asks and allows the grand laying down—the great death—of some of our greatest dreams, He knows best. We say these words, we share them with friends, but they are hard lived when we're staring at the grave of something we're sure wasn't meant to die.

We think we know how to do something big, and God makes it small. We think that all we have is weak and small, and God makes it big.[5]

Surrender: the death of my ideals and dreams can actually mean the beginning of seeing and hearing God's for my life.

But death, first, requires grief. Our tears may necessarily water the path for this surrender.

———— *For Your Continued Pursuit* ————

Psalm 6:3 | Psalm 10:1 | Psalm 18:30 | Psalm 22:1 | Psalm 23 | Psalm 38:9–11 | Psalm 130:1 | Psalm 131:1–2 | Isaiah 26:3 | Isaiah 55:8–9 | John 1:14 | John 12:24 | Romans 5:3–5 | Philippians 4:6–7 | Hebrews 4:12 | Revelation 3:20

---

5. John Piper, *The Hidden Smile of God: The Fruit of Affliction in the Lives of John Bunyan, William Cowper, and David Brainerd* (Wheaton, IL: Crossway, 2001), 19.

6

GOOD GRIEF!

The Power of Grief to Grow Our Surrender

> Heaven knows we never need to be ashamed of our tears, for they are rain upon the blinding dust of earth, overlying our hard hearts.
>
> —CHARLES DICKENS, *GREAT EXPECTATIONS*

I WAS THIRTY-TWO WHEN MY DAD DIED.

Naturally, there was an accepted time and space for grieving at the beginning. Others in my world allowed for it. They expected it. Believers understand this kind of loss.

But then, six years later, as the tears continued to fall and the reality of a fatherless life felt more weighty, it all felt awkwardly out of time and wrong, even. How was I to explain this to friends? I chastised myself for being so self-indulgent. *My life doesn't have time for this,* I insisted. Still, I felt moody, and the grief felt ill timed.

As a culture, we know how to manage certain kinds of loss, and there is a socially acceptable amount of time allowed for that grief. But what about when a career halts, a dream dies, or a friendship is abruptly ended? What about the back injury with no reprieve or the relentless marriage strife? We offer awkward platitudes and quick words of advice, but our hearts often whisper, *Get on with it already*. We speak God's words to another in pain, but we fall well short of adopting his posture. He is near when we grieve—comforting, not looking away or at His watch—yet we humans put an expiration date on pain, a timeline on when things need to wrap up.

Early in our adoption process, when loved ones witnessed the hiccups and bumps that came as our children integrated into our home, they would say, "Oh, that's just all kids."

Sometimes we believed them, and sometimes we responded to the knots in our stomachs that said, *There's something bigger going on in their hearts here. They haven't had a normal childhood.*

But in some instances, we carried the same impatience toward our children's grief that others might have. We overlooked the terror that must have entered into tiny hearts snatched from their home country and placed into the arms of strangers they were now to call Mom and Dad.

We expected an expiration date on their grief.

Mostly we did this because grief felt scary to us. To look at loss felt self-indulgent. "Who has time for that?" we ask as we coach ourselves with Scripture, saying, "I don't want to be offended by God, ungrateful for the things He *has* done, acting like a spoiled child." Nobody wants to live with a smile on her face and a cynical and angry heart, but that's what many of us settle for in our mad dash to "healing." When we put on the facade in the name of being unoffendable, we fail to realize that the ones who genuinely walk unoffended are the ones who grieve their losses and then truly heal because they experienced God holding their hearts through their grief.

But we often skip these hard steps in the interest of the timeline of our ideals. A lifetime of skipping steps makes us resentful of the limits of our humanity—limits that God gives and allows—and resentful of the boundary of the fence line.

As someone prone to hit the road running before the foot fracture has had time to heal, I see how we have built entire theologies to cover over what we dare not admit: we are afraid of pain. We do not know who He is in our darkest hour, the hour handcrafted to touch and make new our deepest places more than anything else.

So we skip over grief.

We skip mourning the loss of a friend or the child who has turned their back on us or the whispers spoken behind our backs. The friend who moved out of town and the summer spent in a sling and the child who chose a different path than we wanted for them. The end of an era at a church and the closed door on the dream job and the broken relationship we thought would result in marriage.

Most of us swiftly move on from the things that could be touchstones in our stories, reminders that God is who He says He is, but we can find that faith only through the gift of grieving. Not one of our losses, no matter how small, is hidden from His sight, and grieving well allows us to move from being a squirmy child in God's lap to becoming one quite comfortable there. Because grieving unearths our need to be held in the dark. God sees even our flash moments of darkness.

In hopping right out of His lap, right out of grief and our need to be held there, we might keep pace with the world (even the Christian world), at least for a while. But we lose what grief is supposed to give us. It's not true that we become less through loss— unless we allow the loss to make us less, grinding our souls until there is nothing left. Loss can also make us more.[1] It can give us part of our inheritance in God.

That inheritance is this: "Blessed are those who mourn, for they will be comforted" (Matt. 5:4 NASB).

You get the comfort of God when you grieve. This is not small.

We work so hard not to experience loss. We do all sorts of acrobatics in our minds and with our actions to ensure that loss isn't the end of this part of our stories, but what if loss is also a beginning?

In grief, you get the arms of God. You get His shared tears on your cheek. You feel His heartbeat against your head as you collapse into His chest. A profound relief comes with grief, the kind I'm living as I'm writing and grieving afresh a new loss in my life.

It's inconvenient to pause the "mission" of our lives to weep. There's a good reason why we don't grieve. But the alternative is a life that evades grief at every turn rather than finding its gold, its power to change our perspective on God. Its ability to finally (finally) dismantle fear. Its potential to fold us into His chest, to make a child out of us.

Children who frequently find safety in their fathers' laps tend to trust the most.

A heart settling into peace with its limitations has found genuine trust in God.

When my dad died, I didn't need someone to tell me how to grieve. I just did. Like when a child learns to walk, instinct overrules teaching. Grief rushes the threshold as a wild man, not a gentleman; it

---

1. Jerry Sittser, *A Grace Disguised: How the Soul Grows through Loss*, revised and expanded (Grand Rapids: Zondervan, 2021), 101.

intrudes during outings with friends, during family dinners, in the checkout line. It doesn't come and then leave forever. Grief is cyclical. We can grieve and find relief only to realize months or years later there is more pain left to tend to.

Every year, a few friends remember the anniversary of my dad's death, and some days, with the warm chai they deliver to my hand, I cry behind my sunglasses, and others, planning for dinner and putting away the dishes, I receive their memorial with gratitude and a steady heart, distracted and not sad. I can't make myself miss my dad on days I don't, and on days that I do, I no longer try to stop.

But as time passed, I learned I *could* put a cork in my grief. I could easily distract myself, eat chocolate, and fill my space with mindless things if I chose not to grieve on that day.

We judge our griefs harshly if we decide that few warrant real tears. Weep over the loss of a parent, but not for years on end. Ache over a move or a job change, sure, but not over the endless weeks that flu works its way through your family. Cry over a house fire and your damaged keepsakes, but not over one more issue that surfaces when you lack the funds to cover your car repairs. Lament a friend's husband's infidelity, and all that means for her, but not the coldness you feel at night when you share a bed with one who won't share his heart with you.

All the minor aches that "don't warrant" more than a moment of grief accrue until they surface through subtle cynicism, bitterness, and jealousy. Some of us coach ourselves with Scripture we don't allow to touch our aching hearts—it merely penetrates our minds—and we still come out dissatisfied.

We often manhandle the minor grievances of life like this until it becomes a habit. Pushed into a darkened corner of our minds, drowned out by noise, relegated to the bottom of a never-ending to-do list—unthinking, we suffocate our sobs and talk ourselves out of tears.

Several people in my life, including some of my children, lost their parents in their early years. Many of them learned slick methods for evading that grief. How is a five-year-old to handle the loss of their dad without someone to sit with them in that grief or lacking the wherewithal to field something so significant alone? Many of them became master evaders. They had to. How could they not have? The grief was overwhelming for their tiny frames to face alone.

Many of us learned to field our hearts' scrapes and bruises similarly. We became master evaders, whether for lack of adults or friends around us who could hold a tissue and let us cry, or for lack of felt safety despite those holding a tissue. Even at young ages, we learned to turn on the television, turn to a screen, buy another pair of shoes, renovate another area of our homes, or fill our time with friends and activities and loud laughter—to hide what we deemed to be insignificant hurts.

Over time, little escapes lead to well-formed habits. We manage the pain that felt as if it had nowhere to go or no one to hold it. We develop theologies around the avoidance of pain, thinking surely God is as impatient with us as we are with our friends who still keep hurting over the same aches in their lives.

But God doesn't avoid pain. A well-worn children's book wedged into the wooden bin of books in our family room tells us, "Can't go over it! Can't go under it! Can't go around it! Gotta go through it."[2] So it goes with Jesus of Calvary. He, too, requested a reprieve from the pain: "Father, if you are willing, take this cup from me" (Luke 22:42).

---

2. Helen Oxenbury, *Going on a Bear Hunt* (New York: Little Simon, 1997).

But it's the valley, the cross, the end of us wherein the beginning of Him lies.

Psalm 34:18 says, "The LORD is close to the brokenhearted and saves those who are crushed in spirit." A variation of this is written in Psalm 147:3: "He heals the brokenhearted and binds up their wounds."

Skipping the step of grieving even life's minor paper cuts exempts us from experiencing Jesus' nearness—the lines on His face, the tenderness in His voice, the feel of His calluses across our tear-streaked faces. Skipping the step of grieving prevents us from a measure of healing we'll never know.

All the while, God's invitation remains the same: *Come to me. With your tiredness, your overwhelm, your sadness over what you thought this season would be. Come to me. Come to me with lowercase aches, the ones your dad might coach you out of or your sister might say are foolish. The ones that don't compare with the child starving in Africa. Come to me with those aches. Yes, come to me when your neighbor has lost their spouse, and when you think it's foolish to cry over another unpaid bill.* God doesn't set us on a scale to see who is crushed enough in spirit to warrant comfort. Many of us have years of splinters we never brought to Him, and we wonder why our hope is lost.

"I don't think I'm going to die hopeless, but I might spend a good year here."

I sent the text to two old friends who used to call me by my maiden name, who'd seen me wear my first pair of Birkenstocks— the ones on which I painted daisies—when I was sixteen. They knew me well enough to know I wasn't tossing my faith, but this was a new low for me.

You see, grief is not a one-and-done. Some losses revisit us in stages and seasons, haunting us with what is not, haunting our memory with the dissonance between what is real and what we dreamed would be. Like a dear friend who lost her mom at a young age; each milestone in life brought grief. She didn't grow out of grief.

Nor did I.

And some griefs have layers.

Something told me in this new stage of grief—over a loss too profound to write in pages other than my journal—that I had to remain hopeless for a while before finding hope for this situation. I had to sit in the dark. Experience and His Word reminded me that grief has a course, like a rambling river carving a path and ever so slightly but steadily altering earth in its way. Surrender will come, but tears are to carve a way. And sometimes those tears need to be shed for months and years before surrender happens.

I thought it was grief that was wearying, but grief was the beginning of a reprieve. Was I tired from all the hurting in our home? *Yes.* Was I tired from the sheer number of mouths to feed? *Yes.* Was I tired from the responsibility that felt too big for me to carry? *Yes.* But the most profound wearying agent was my way of navigating all the outcomes. I was bone tired from steering my course, from living for specific outcomes and mitigating against others. It's an exhausting way to live, yet most of us do so unthinkingly. Just as casually as we brush our teeth, we hedge our bets.

But now, it was as if I had burrowed down to the real grief: I was grieving my disposition and the way of relating to the world that had gotten me to where I was. I wasn't grieving the fence line. I was bemoaning how I related to it, which led to exhaustion.

God took His time in the uncovering.

God is not in a hurry.

He wasn't in a hurry for me to hope like I might have rushed my friends to hope when we were all in our early thirties and struggling. He was initiating me into the reprieve of grief—the grief that takes time to make a way into the heart.

He doesn't mind the darkness. "Darkness is as light" to him (Ps. 139:12).

So I answered my friends' texts "How are you?" with a promise not to stay in hopelessness forever but to stay as long as I needed—as evidence of baby steps of trust and finding a new way.

"A life of prayer forces us to deal with the reality of the world and of our own lives at a depth and with an honesty that is quite unheard of by the prayerless, and much of that reality we would certainly avoid if we could."[3]

To talk to God, we must first believe that language is a language of the heart. Sure, He cares deeply about our cross-country moves, our recent job changes, and who we will marry, but there are thousands of thoughts and decisions between life's most significant moments.

The friend who walked past you on the soccer sidelines to gather with the other moms. The dentist bill you didn't expect, sitting on the counter now for weeks. The child who still can't read. The small group to which you weren't invited.

Prayer can start with grief. Loss. All the things you have subconsciously talked yourself out of feeling might be fodder for growing your deepest conversation with God.

Our road with God includes many deaths. We were promised

3. Eugene Peterson, *Answering God: The Psalms as Tools for Prayer* (San Francisco: HarperOne, 1989), 121.

85

to lose our lives, and yet we fight this. The death that God invites us into is not a mortification of all desire or a squelching of the childhood dreams He put within us; it is an exchange. An exchange that often gives us clarity about our dreams and desires. And, sometimes, we (finally) let things die that we were sure shouldn't, in order to receive the life He has in store for us. It is not true to say that God wants to teach us something in our trials. Through every cloud, He wants us to *unlearn* something.[4]

But there is still death. And death without grief leaves latent, unnamed emotions not brought before God powerfully invisible inside us.

The God who created emotions invites us to grieve them with Him. But really, He invites us to be held as we grieve.

And this is the process of surrender.

I will never outgrow the need for a touch from God, but sometimes life has weathered me enough that I stop looking for it.

I forget what it felt like to be fifteen and on my back-porch swing at nightfall in June when He might as well have been sitting beside me. He felt so near.

So many years between then and now.

So much loss—my dad, my little-girl dreams, the naivete of the '90s, when we listened to Caedmon's Call and were sure the world was only getting better. Leaning away from idealism and the youthful thrill of one-hit wonders with God also put me at risk of seeing life in two tones. Oh, the tension of choosing that long and quiet

---

4. Oswald Chambers, *My Utmost for His Highest* (Grand Rapids: Our Daily Bread, 2017), July 29.

obedience (which often happens over time, as we grow in God), finding God in the shadowed corners, and yet still falling asleep praying for an instant miracle.

Nate and I spent one of our anniversaries in the Tetons. And there God met me, like when I was fifteen on my back-porch swing, but He met the grown version of me, so that meeting had greater substance.

We stayed in a two-bedroom French provincial cabin owned by a woman from France. An hour outside of Jackson Hole and on the Idaho side, it felt like the middle of nowhere, but "nowhere" included a sunrise over the Tetons that shot fiery colors across the sky, and hummingbirds playing in the lavender just outside the kitchen window. Scuffed wooden floors showed years of life underneath the farmhouse table, but our days there held quiet living. We slept with the windows open, awoke to 50 degrees in August, and swung on the well-loved wooden swing set out back.

This all would have been enough for a heart that had gotten used to finding Him in the worn edges and the tired furniture. I suppose that made it the perfect timing for a miracle. (I used to think I had to watch and pray with eyes wide open so as not to miss the miraculous. But more recently, I believe He shows off when we least expect it.)

This miracle wasn't loud. It was a miracle of the heart, in my chest, one I'll remember for decades, I'm sure. I'd been round and round several circumstances where the invitation continued to surface: *Let me, Sara. Let me hold. Let me handle it.*

On the last day of our trip, I couldn't verbalize the anxiety or fear that surfaced as I considered life back home, the life with the continual ache that a trip away wouldn't forever clear, but I have learned that the knots in my stomach and the racing of my heart tell me what my mind won't. We came to Jenny Lake, an enormous glacier lake tucked away in Grand Teton National Park, to take a trip across it and hike up the mountain surrounding it. Nate was expectant, and I was knotted up on the inside—apparently I couldn't leave issues back in Kansas City.

After a ferry ride across the lake, we started our hike, and something inside reminded me: start small. I said to God, *I think I need to be held.*

Immediately I saw in my mind our Virginia, then five years old—her wild hair and tender heart. ("I'm the tenderest one in our family, Mommy," she would often tell me.) She is a tiny version of me, full of feelings and often overwhelmed by them. Now I was her, holding out my hand, anxious, troubled by the same things that had bothered me for some time and needing a dad. I pictured Him gently holding my hand.

It was simple, but it was overpowering.

For a minute I felt His hand more than I felt my fear.

I didn't coach myself not to be anxious—a frequent response to my anxieties, big and small. I just felt His fingers, bigger than mine, sure, fixed.

Dozens of times, I prayed this prayer on our hike—letting myself envision my hand being held—up the steep inclines where Nate and I were breathing too heavily to talk and as we looked out across the expanse of the Tetons, navigating wildflowers and mountain creeks and waterfalls.

Dozens of times, I felt the surety of His hand. Sometimes it was wrapped around mine, sometimes on the small of my back, always meeting my skittish heart just as I needed.

Peace came in His hand on the small of my back and wrapped around my little-girl fingers.

Peace came in the small receiving of His reach toward me.

Nate and I have our hiking rhythm. We're swift on the uphill, heaving and heart racing, and a bit competitive to the peak. We talk very little on the way up. The downhill is for stopping, breathing mountain air and noticing our breath, praying, laughing, talking about all the things we can't discuss under the constant interruption of life with seven kids. We meander our way down the mountain every time.

On this hike, I had a lump in my throat for much of the way down. This hike had been different after I felt the touch of God. Instead of being distracted in my thoughts, I was enraptured by the views. Wild flowers were vibrant, the rush of the mountain streams exhilarating. The marmots ducking and hiding in the rock crevices, and the snap of the grasshoppers captured my attention. I didn't look away to escape my thoughts as I often do. I was present, engaged with the mountain sounds and smells. Receiving.

I grew in trust that day, just a trembling little girl, too little to coach herself, but big enough to ask for a hand to hold.

And the more I trust, the more I see.

Sure, today still holds a little anxiety about these things, and so will tomorrow. The miracle still needs to be worn in and put on daily. But He gave me a glimpse of the way through.

On the last pass down the mountain before we caught the ferry back, we saw a bull moose about fifteen feet from us. I'd been looking for him on every mountain trip I could remember, and, of course, we saw him this day. Miracles on the inside. Miracles on the outside.

Surrender is the sigh of life. It's the moment—surely you have experienced it once or twice—when His Holy Spirit overshadows and you're able to say, "Not my will, but yours, Lord." It's the unclenched fist, the little-girl prayer, the simplicity of letting go, which is also one of the most complicated parts of our walk with God. Surrender is fiercely powerful for the human soul, and yet it sometimes comes in a whisper, a kick of dust at the gravesite, a mere moment when what felt to be an immovable part of us we could now relinquish.

Surrender makes a child out of me and you. It turns grown men into young boys still needing to be fathered. Surrender reimagines the fence line. It is no longer an electric fence buzzing ominously but rather just a line on the horizon, and we are fixed on the freedom we feel within that space. It makes strong women pigtailed and carefree. Surrender invites the peace of soul that is evidenced in a life that trusts, a life that says, *I'll die to me, God, so that I can have You.* Surrender is wildly supernatural and often comes after thousands of small steps in one direction.

It's when you realize your grown child will make their own decisions, many of them separate from you, and your heart is at rest. It's the job you didn't get and the quiet of the night where you'd otherwise be heart-racing and tracing the ceiling with your eyes, but you fall asleep in peace because something inside of you knows: *It's better His way.*

Surrender is when I've made dozens of attempts in a week to reach a child whose history predates me, whose history makes them leery of trusting, cautious about receiving love, and I welcome the whisper in my heart, *You were never meant to be enough for them.* No parent is. And I settle into being a mother to seven whose needs I can't all meet. I settle into that thought rather than resisting or building a life, a schedule, or a plan against it. I surrender to it.

As George MacDonald said, "With every morn my life afresh

must break."[5] And when I let it, when I let Him break it, He gives me His peace in exchange. And the night—the dark—becomes where I fall asleep in His peace.

Surrender comes when we travel the cross with Him. Surrender must include a dark Friday's death and a heavy Saturday mourning before the brilliant revealing of Sunday's resurrection is not just a thought in our heads but a deep, sighing, breathing reality that forms our lives.

And grief—where I bring my broken dreams, big and small, to the burial site and put them in the ground, with Him at my side, patiently healing me as I grieve—gives way to surrender.

Surrender: my life, my dreams, my expectations, my plans. For His.

——— *For Your Continued Pursuit* ———

Psalm 18:11 | Psalm 34:18 | Psalm 139:11–12 | Psalm 147:3 | Isaiah 30:15 | Matthew 5:4 | Matthew 11:28–30 | Matthew 16:25 | Luke 1:38 | Luke 9:23–25 | Luke 22:42 | Romans 6:1–11 | 2 Corinthians 1:3–4

---

5. George MacDonald, *Diary of an Old Soul* (Mansfield Centre, CT: Martino Publishing, 2015), Oct. 10.

7

BEAUTIFUL
BOUNDARY LINES

> I have come home at last! This is my real country! I
> belong here. This is the land I have been looking for
> all my life, though I never knew it till now.
> —C. S. LEWIS, *THE LAST BATTLE*

GOD OFTEN REACHES US THROUGH WHAT WE SEE IN
front of us.

The night before our twenty-first wedding anniversary, I
received a text from Nate while I was away writing. "Well, the ceiling just collapsed."

We'd noticed water dripping through the ceiling fan in our
boys' bedroom for weeks before then. We could never quite pinpoint
the leak. It was so small and intermittent and dispersed through the
fan that for a while we thought Bo was sloppy with his drinking
water while kicking the wall and reading his book cockeyed on his
bed. (Eight-year-old boys are pretty gifted with simple things like
water and fire and charcoal.)

Once we'd determined it was a leak, even though it was the middle of an arid August, we contacted professionals. *It must be the air-conditioning unit.* They assured us there was nothing wrong, and yet the leak continued.

With two trips planned for that August and then preparing for the start of school, we mostly forgot this insignificant leak after that. Then one afternoon Bo discovered another leak, farther from the fan and along a ceiling seam. Nate called the company that had just installed solar panels on our roof. They discovered they'd accidentally kicked out a pipe connected to the air-conditioning unit in the ceiling. Our attic had been fielding gallons of water since we first spotted the leak. As if on cue, that same afternoon more water drips emerged from different parts of the ceiling, so much so that we began to see a bulge. Hours later, the ceiling gave way. Piles of insulation filled our boys' room. Sock drawers, schoolbooks, and bins of Lincoln Logs now held wet, matted insulation. They could look from their beds into the attic—every boy's dream and every parent's waking nightmare.

Our home was a revolving door for six weeks, welcoming water cleanup crews, mold mitigation teams, drywall installers, and painters. We were handed a home reconstruction project because of a tiny error.

A friend said casually, "The things that happen in and to my home have tended to reflect the work of God in my heart." Her phrase stuck with me as I chose new paint colors, ordered new beds for the boys, and fielded the inspection report.

This was the same August as our miraculous time at Jenny Lake and the hike during which God held my hand. It was the same summer I'd felt for months that its season of grieving was coming to a close and that surrender was near. Though the process of grief is not often that linear, this particular summer it was. I'd been invited to grieve, chosen to sit in pain when I'd rather shop or reorganize my home, and I felt I'd walked through the valley with this ache, and its time was coming to a close.

Then my ceiling collapsed.

Ceilings, like walls, create a room. We know the boundaries of the room by its four walls and its eight- or nine- or ten-foot upward expanse. Ceilings limit, just like fence lines. I can't see the sky in my bedroom. I'm also protected from the rain. The floor of my boys' room is my ceiling, where my space ends and theirs begins.

Much of what I needed to grieve in the months before the ceiling collapsed were my white-knuckle dreams, the things I desperately wanted for my family and my children. I kept reaching toward those ideals, again, the little-girl dreamer needing to be held by God. More sophisticated ideals became like gravity, pulling me toward dreams that don't include God and keep me from having honest conversations with Him.

So there I was, from spring through summer, naming the subterranean pain, choosing not to try to fix my circumstances or get myself out of that hurt, and grieving this moment of loss.

In August I'd felt a lifting, finally—one I could attribute only to the hand of God, the Holy Spirit, helping me to let go, to surrender.

Was the ceiling's collapse an exclamation point to my internal life, perhaps?

C. S. Lewis said, "There are also all sorts of things in our own spiritual life, where a thing has to be killed, and broken, in order that it may then become bright and strong and splendid."[1]

There is a process between the dozens of collapses that happen across a lifetime and the rebuilt structures that come from them. Just as time doesn't heal all wounds, surrender won't come without

---

1. C. S. Lewis, *God in the Dock* (Grand Rapids: Eerdmans, 2014), 79.

our participation, and so we can't receive the fruit of surrender unless we are actively involved. This surrender is a choice, though, and it is rarely made as tidily as Hallmark would have us believe.

And surrender, like grief, is cyclical. Across a lifetime, we revisit patches of ground that need tilling and new seeds.

"The LORD is my chosen portion and my cup; you hold my lot. The lines have fallen for me in pleasant places; indeed, I have a beautiful inheritance" (Ps. 16:5–6 ESV).

This verse speaks to aspirations that feel far from my reality. Hand-lettered on my wall or crocheted and displayed in Grandma's kitchen, what this verse says can feel distant from what we experience and how we relate to Him. We want to feel this, to know this, to claim it as true for our hearts, but many of us subconsciously feel disappointed with our portions, our lots. We don't like the lines God has given us.

Our youngest son, Bo, has been raised among teenagers. At ages seven and eight, Bo went to bed long before his siblings returned home. Looking at them, he sees friendship as coffee dates and movie nights and capture the flag in the back yard in the pitch dark. He peeks over the fence line as he shares a bedroom and a kitchen with siblings double his age. While the child can lose himself for hours building forts in the woods and can spend an entire afternoon building his Lego sets, he still asks for a coffee date with a friend or a late party so he and his buddies can play football in the moonlight.

He is me, and he is you. It's simple for me to see that Bo, at eight, has necessary limits that let him thrive because he did not eat sugar and drink soda before bed and had a good night of sleep. But I sometimes think I have aged out of these limits. I equate adulthood with limitlessness and forget that God limited Himself when He placed His Son inside Mary's frame.

But Psalm 16:5–6 is not an unobtainable aspiration for us eight-at-hearters. It becomes real on the other side of surrender, on the other side of mourning and loss.

As is true for most of life, just listening to sermons will not get us there; we need to experience the Word climbing into our story and speaking to our hearts' cries and reviving us when we need new breath.

Eugene Peterson said, "Every Christian story is a freedom story. Each story tells how a person has been set free from the confines of small ideas, from the chains of what others think, from the prisons of the self, sin-separated from God. We are free to change. The process of that change is always a good story but is never a neat formula."[2]

The slow unfurling of our fingers from what we were certain our lives would look like at a given stage gives way to our holding the radiant beauty of God's story, written and read through us. The end of me initiates the beginning of Him. "Whoever loses their life . . . will find it" (Matt. 16:25).

In *The Last Battle*, C. S. Lewis describes heaven in this way: "The land I have been looking for all my life, though I never knew it till now."[3]

We are intended for a homecoming, a coming into ourselves, a return to what we've always craved. A settling, but into arms, not a

---

2. Eugene Peterson, *As Kingfishers Catch Fire* (Colorado Springs: WaterBrook, 2019), 289.

3. C. S. Lewis, *The Last Battle* (New York: Harper Collins, 1956), 196.

dwelling. Settling into a person—the home we've longed for, the one we spend most of our days searching for, unknowingly. We search for home in friendships and community and church and work. We search for a sense of belonging and a settledness into a place that is so clearly ours—that unwaveringly receives us as we are—through our kids in their relationships, connectedness in community, achievements, and being accepted and received. But deep in our souls, we know that kind of connection is unattainable this side of heaven, and the gift of limitations becomes clear when we look for another way to quench the longing inside of us for home.

It's here—at the end of our search for home in people and relationships and accomplishments—that He gives us another world, the one we always wanted, the one in the looking glass where we see shades of green in the grass blades and notice the variegations the sky holds on a summer day. A world that is better because it's unfalteringly home.

And it's inside the fence line.

It takes unaccountable effort to pursue life on the other side of the fence—to pursue the dream, the ideal, the limitless life. The tiredness I felt in my bones that, for years, I attributed to my number of children or to walking some of them through the pain of healing from trauma, I now revisit with curiosity. Was it more my reaching for something that wasn't mine to have that made me so tired?

The vigilance, the wielding of circumstances and situations to quiet the places in me that felt uncomfortable with my limits required more energy than I had, more energy than I was made to have.

"Watchful, not vigilant."

The phrase came to me one morning in the shower as I was praying. Those two words are nearly interchangeable per Webster, but they carried a different weight in my mind.

Vigilance reminded me about the early years following our adoptions. One of our children could seemingly hear conversations from two rooms away not because of exceptional hearing but because of a lifestyle of vigilant insecurity—expectant in the hardest of ways, as if expecting loss might mitigate the pain: what you see coming can't hurt you as much as a surprise attack can. The parentless develop their own skills to survive.

But that kind of vigilance isn't exclusive to the once orphaned.

Many of us have mastered it accidentally.

We read the facial expressions of our employers or read between the lines of their emails, doing all sorts of mental gymnastics to win praise or dodge disapproval.

We know our spouses' hot spots and tiptoe around them, vigilant to avoid conflict.

We assess the new small group, the new church, or the new Bible study for what they value, exercising vigilant observation and subtly working to adhere to those things.

We speculate about texts and intonations, invitations or the lack thereof, preparing ourselves to be omitted, unneeded, unwanted.

And then there's my particular poison: dread.

I've known it since I was young. I'm so familiar with it that I almost overlook the deepest layers of this form of vigilance.

A child shows early signs of sickness, and, unthinking, I begin adjusting our schedule for many days ahead to accommodate. A teenager struggles and I unconsciously anticipate facing a rift in our relationship ten years later. The persistent headache, the drip underneath the sink, the downturn in the economy—they all have future implications in my mind. And so I am subject to a future world in my head that isn't the reality in front of me. Because I still resent my limitations, I dread the potential of more.

But the thing about dread for us believers is that it isn't a placeholder or something we should live with.

Dread occupies the same space where our God-given imagination is meant to reside.

In Ephesians, Paul prays this for the saints who are in Ephesus: "That the God of our Lord Jesus Christ, the Father of glory, may give to you the spirit of wisdom and revelation in the knowledge of Him, the eyes of your understanding being enlightened; that you may know what is the hope of His calling, what are the riches of the glory of His inheritance in the saints, and what is the exceeding greatness of His power toward us who believe" (Eph. 1:17–19 NKJV).

In Greek, the word *understanding* means "imagination." Paul is praying that ones like you and me would have our imagination set aflame with the hope of God and our inheritance in Him.

But dread is the killjoy of our imagination. It occupies the same space as imagination in our minds and hearts but is the darkened version of it. And vigilance is dread's carrier through our minds and deep into our hearts.

So that night, as I prayed for God to restore and renew my mind, this new thought that dropped into my head felt much like an invitation: be watchful instead of vigilant.

You see, hypervigilance around any impending struggle or strife makes us singleminded, focused exclusively on contingency plans. Vigilance demands a lack of sleep, an ever-alertness, a habitual state of being on guard for every eventuality. Of course we're exhausted, vigilantly guarding what we want to be ours, vigilantly pursuing a life that doesn't limit us.

But to be watchful is to simply see.

To see with curiosity. To see with the trust of a child, watching the show and imagining a good ending. To see what we don't know but our hearts crave. To be watchful is to have eyes open to God, all around, always working.

I can watch God light the sky on fire at dusk and lift a small part of my heart. (And that sky fire will happen whether I see it or not.)

I can see a teenager's heart unfurl with a single phrase, dripping with vulnerability and openness to God and trust. (I could hear that phrase as background noise but not receive it as a sign of God's work.)

I can see Nate holding a tender son, whispering in his ear of his delight and take it as commonplace, or I can remember that gruff twenty-four-year-old I married and marvel that God gave him much more than merely a salt-and-pepper beard in his second half of life.

I can slide my glasses on to read a text of encouragement from a friend that speaks to one of my biggest insecurities and then swipe left for the next task, or I can watch that moment as if God gave it in order to reach me.

God wants us to imagine a life where His power is potent, where we see Him in the sky fire and our hearts are awakened, where relationships don't just die in bitterness, where fathers and sons are restored to one another, where marriages animate inside His glory. Yes, even in our suffering, sorrowful times He wants us to imagine a life where we feel entrusted to Him in our darkest hours. (This last one, alone, is no minor miracle.)

And this godly imagination comes as we exchange our plans and dreams for His.

Philippians 2:8–10 says of Jesus, "And being found in appearance as a man, He humbled Himself and became obedient to the point of death, even the death of the cross. Therefore God also has highly exalted Him and given Him the name which is above every name, that at the name of Jesus every knee should bow, of those in heaven, and of those on earth, and of those under the earth" (NKJV).

Therefore.

There was a *therefore*, even for Jesus. He, too, had this exchange. A dark Friday night. A cup of which He asked to be relieved (Luke 22:42). A death that required obedience. An end.

And then God's unfolding story. Jesus' exaltation. His being given a name that brought glory to God and bowed knees to the Father, a name that healed and set people free and made God known.

While more dramatic and undoubtedly perfect compared with our potholed and winding road, Jesus' dark Friday night and Saturday mourning meant a story and a life that made God known and set man free.

This exchange is available to us. Potent power and beauty, minutes that are enflamed with God, waking up in peace and falling asleep in peace. Surely there is sin and strife and nailbiting and chocolate-binging and snapping at those we love, but what would an undercurrent of peace with our lot—our cup, our portion, our inheritance—feel like and look like? Try it on. This is the invitation on the other side of relinquishing our tightfisted grip on the limitless life we envision.

Watchful, not vigilant: there's just too much to see out there.

Tim Keller said, "We are God's priority. To each of us he says, 'What in my life is more important than you?'"[4]

---

4. Tim Keller, *First John Leader's Guide* (New York: Redeemer Presbyterian Church, 2007), 30–31.

These are the words we spend our energy reaching to hear. Behind our incessant drive for others to receive us, to win at the tasks in front of us, to be noticed in some measure and be included, to be enfolded into family is a drive to be someone's priority. To find a forever home in someone we trust. And much of our adult lives are God hedging us so that we might finally see only one someone, only one family that will not disappoint, only one home that is forever safe.

Our limits are purposed, not accidental. We push past them to find what we're craving, but God can develop in us a much smaller push for more significant things, a push that starts with our eyes.

Watchfulness. It enables us to enter the story, whether fielding our losses, letting ourselves grieve them, or breathing the sigh of surrender that says, "Your story, God, not mine."

Watchfulness—on the back end of the cycle of loss, grief, and surrender we inevitably work our way through dozens of times in our lives—can be full of wonder. Watchfulness can make us children again, finding the treasure of home.

Once on my Saturday-morning drive home from the gym, I decided to turn off the music—no voice memos to friends or podcasts, either. I'd been choosing to sit in silence a bit more often, noticing that my body, mind, and heart were more tired than I had assessed.

On this Saturday, my heart felt expectant. It was the same summer of grief and surrender bleeding into the same fall of our ceiling collapse. It seemed all these things carved a little more space and capacity for me to sit in silence before God without discomfort. I was becoming more comfortable choosing watchfulness over vigilance regarding the details of my life. So I turned off the noise from my phone and rolled down the windows to absorb the sounds and colors outside my car.

Within a minute, I saw two flitting monarchs move from one end of my windshield to the other. I could barely enjoy these two before I saw another, and another, then two more. If they had been higher up in the sky, I would have imagined them to be twos and threes of distant birds. But they were monarchs, more of them. And still more. I stopped counting at thirty.

Cars raced around me on this four-lane road, focused drivers headed to Lowe's or their sons' soccer games or a Saturday runners meet-up at the park. Their music was loud and their eyes were glazed, like mine often are—not in the *selah* of the moment but already mentally in the next. Had it been yesterday, I wouldn't have noticed a butterfly. Perhaps they *were* there yesterday and I missed them on this familiar road, mind bent toward task and calendar item. No one around me appeared to notice the parade of monarchs on display.

This was watchfulness. God was teaching me. It's a seventeen-minute drive to my gym, and many days I don't know what happened during those seventeen minutes. Seventeen minutes of ruminating about my life or planning the next task or frozen in a mental loop that tires me. But this day, He was teaching me watchfulness: within my reach is a world full of beauty and story and whispers of God, waiting to make this day rich and different from the last and different from the next. The monotony of morning rhythms and teaching littles their letters and big kids to drive and serving meal after meal after meal is continuously interrupted by a wonder He is offering me. But when my eyes are locked on what I can't have, on what this season isn't, on where I am not, on what may come that might hinder me, I have no room for watchfulness.

Paul encourages us: "I say, walk by the Spirit, and you will not gratify the desires of the flesh" (Gal. 5:16). This concept can feel big and ethereal, out of reach. But His Spirit helps us when we can't get our minds around what it might mean to walk by the Spirit. He meets us where we are and in small ways. With a whisper—like the butterfly—saying, *Find me here. Home is here, where I am.*

Saturdays are a bit more free range in our home. Teenagers spread their homework across tabletops and counters and stay in their pajamas extra long. Schoolbooks litter our first floor as their flitting attention takes up more space than they do during the week. The littlest ones, hair unbrushed and wild, don't have the same structure that Monday through Friday affords. And if they are on Dad's watch, they have pajamas and snacks all day too. Nate tackles his honey-do list and the lawn, and I try to tie up loose ends from the week and plan the upcoming week. In many ways, Saturdays, before our Sunday rest, are my least favorite day of the week. They bring chaos.

But that Saturday drive home from the gym was the picture of life offered in the Spirit—watchful, childlike anticipation. Butterflies on the craziest day of the week. Interruptions to mental roadblocks, heart heaviness, and narratives we have nursed for all our days—this is the life in the Spirit. Jesus whispers. His Word interrupts our thoughts. Beauty and silence and diversion all as part of His story.

These things are happening all around us. Each morning the heavens are declaring a story of God, a story different from the one of lack or heaviness, discouragement and dread. Every day there is another story being told—this is life in the Spirit—but I have a choice. Will I choose His story? The limitless nature of what He's offering me? Or will I choose to stare at my limits, to study the fence line, to compare myself with others who have different boundaries than me?

The mind set on the Spirit—this life of the Spirit coursing through waking and sleeping, decisions and relationships—is life and peace (Rom. 8:6).

Home: my life, my sense of my limitations, my experience of the fence line offered to Him in exchange for His home—the home He made for me, in Him. He gives me a home. He settles me inside my limitations with promises of the limitlessness that is to come and that is right now, within Him. I'm held in the home of His making, breathing a sigh of relief after setting aside my exhausted living and receiving the gift of His light and airy home.

This is radical and it's counter to everything in my being and it's exactly what I was made for. I am home in His story and home in myself.

Come (choose to step forward and not stay stuck), die (let Him have His way with you), grieve (collapse into God, and don't forget your thwarted longings when you do), and live (truly live) unto greater trust, unto finding a home. Again and again and again.

——— *For Your Continued Pursuit* ———

Psalm 16:5–6 | Psalm 19:1 | Psalm 113:9 | Psalm 119:125 | Matthew 11:28–30 | Matthew 16:25 | Luke 22:42 | John 14:26–28 | Romans 8:6 | Romans 12:2 | Galatians 5:16 | Ephesians 1:17–19 | Philippians 2:5–10 | 1 Peter 4:19

Part 3

GETTING PRACTICAL
Living within Our Limits

WHO DOESN'T WANT TO GET PRACTICAL? I CAN'T GET engrossed in a love story—a novel or a movie—without wanting to wrap my arms around Nate and pull him close. The best ideas are embodied.

Let's put skin on these ideas. The pages ahead are for moving the ethereal into what we can taste, see, touch, smell, and hear. They are for the equipping—for the minute after you close this book today and the years after you slide it onto your bookshelf but bump up against the same limits you had before you read it.

8

THE STORY UNDERNEATH OUR SKIN

> How can you draw close to God when you are far from your own self?
> —AUGUSTINE

I WAS PREGNANT AND HOMEBOUND BECAUSE OF A BROKEN ankle when I heard that my aunts were planning a surprise party for my mom's seventieth birthday. My brain and body, tired from navigating once simple things like cooking and climbing the stairs to tuck little people into bed, while also growing a human inside me and having only one good foot, failed to understand that the party for my mom was actually a *party. Oh, that's nice,* I thought. *They want me to know how they're taking care of her on her birthday.*

My aunt called me to share a date and some details, and somewhere along the line, I imagined her plans as a small-scale, local-family-only backyard barbeque that she was kind enough to mention. I lived three states away, couldn't travel alone with the cast on my ankle, and spent most afternoons sleeping—this baby requiring excessive amounts of my thirty-nine-year-old energy. There was no way to figure out how to attend this potluck that was three weeks away.

Days before my mom's birthday, an uncle (one who lived in a different state than my mom and her sisters who were planning the party) asked for photographs for the slideshow.

Wait, I thought, a lump rising in my throat as the reality set in. *Slideshow?*

The gathering seemed simple and small—at least, I thought that's what it was. *Where will they project this slideshow? And from whom is he gathering photos? And he will be there from out of state?*

Then I learned that several of my mom's siblings were flying in from different states.

My heart sank as my mind absorbed the information I was intended to receive weeks before.

Oh, no. My aunt wasn't merely checking in on me. She was suggesting I *come*.

Of course! A party for my beloved mom where her siblings and my siblings were all gathering. How could I miss this?

And how could I have missed this?

Broken ankle and pregnancy lethargy aside, there was no way now to get a plane ticket, find someone to travel with me, and arrange for coverage for me at home so I could go.

I spent most of the day of her party at home in a fog, distracted. Powerful, unnamed emotions hung like dense clouds over my head. I felt low, sunk, even. This silly ankle injury and how my older body handled pregnancies—my mental fog and slowness and droning fatigue—made this another in a mounting set of nos.

But this one was to my *mom*, the woman who'd spent seven weeks in our home after I birthed my first baby, who learned our daily rhythms and implemented them better than I did, who acted as a refuge for teenage hearts and rounded toddler bodies. Not to mention that I'd be on the outside again. Siblings and family gathered, while our choice to move across the country and have a larger family that sometimes prevented us from traveling with ease kept us from being inside their swirl. Again.

I bit my nails, ate chocolate, and mainly felt grumpy, assuming it was all because I couldn't attend the party.

The storyline in my head on the day of the party was simple: they were all there, but I couldn't go. My mom got celebrated, and I couldn't participate in celebrating her. Wouldn't you be grumpy too? It was uncomplicated. My limitations kept me from caring for my mother on her important day.

But a few days after the party, I started to see the similar hues of limitations of the past. Sure, I was limited by my circumstances, but I was also on the outside. Left out. Being left out felt much more challenging than being limited. Even though I had been invited, I wasn't included. My family formed more memories, took more pictures, and exchanged more inside jokes that didn't include me.

The ache was not merely about being limited, that I couldn't travel on a whim. It wasn't merely that I'd missed the chance to bless my mom. The deeper source of my malaise was feeling excluded.

It is a terrible feeling. Kept from deeper connection, deeper belonging, that figurative sense of home for which we're always reaching—is there a worse hedge?

This wasn't my broken ankle or the missed opportunity. (We celebrated my mom weeks later in ways that came just shy of fireworks.) It wasn't my mom's disappointment in my not being there. (She hardly flinched.) It was my hurting heart.

And once I recognized that, I knew what to bring to God.

Days before, I had been lamenting having a broken ankle and so many children and such a tired body. Those things are still fodder for good conversation with God, but perhaps not as deep-reaching as when I let myself be the little girl standing outside, feeling scared and sad.

Asking God to hold those parts of me—the shaky, insecure, questioning parts—gives Him the opportunity to respond as He always does: quick to comfort, delighting in being near, generous in His connection. It's an opportunity for the shame to lift and for my sense of home in Him to be restored.

We hover around the circumstances that highlight our limitations, mostly unaware of why they make us so anxious, often calling them warfare or merely circumstances, or acting as if they're bad luck, and yet underneath them is what God wants to show us, to tend to with us.

Underneath them, we crave connection.

Jesus said to the woman at the well, "Whoever drinks of the water that I will give him will never be thirsty again" (John 4:14 ESV).

Most of us don't recognize our craving, our thirst. Missing the party showed me mine—the insecure parts that had less to do with why I couldn't get there (my limitations) and more to do with what I wanted inside (belonging, a sense of home).

John Calvin said, "Our wisdom . . . consists almost entirely of two parts: knowledge of God and of ourselves."[1]

We can have the same conversation with God, much like we

---

1. John Calvin, *The Institutes of Christian Religion* (Peabody, MA: Hendrickson, 2008), 4.

have the same argument with our spouses, over and over and over again. Rewind, repeat. And often we name this "stuck," as if God isn't responsive or we're not creative enough to capture His attention. But what if there is a third way?

Paying attention. I take time to notice myself. I notice the fog, rather than pushing through it. I pause to observe—without evaluation and strategy, but simply to understand what might be happening below the surface so that I can bring that understanding into my conversation with God. Paul says in Ephesians 4:22–24, "Put off your old self, which belongs to your former manner of life and is corrupt through deceitful desires, and . . . be renewed in the spirit of your minds, and . . . put on the new self, created after the likeness of God in true righteousness and holiness" (ESV).

At fifteen, I thought following God and putting off my old self meant drinking soda at parties, not alcohol, and "staying pure." I stopped cussing and felt guilty when I tried cigarettes to look cool. Behavioral changes. Clearly I missed the full perspective of this verse, but I wonder whether you, like me, sometimes ask yourself what you're putting off or putting on. Perhaps these verses are an invitation to pause, consider, notice: *What is old in me, God, and what is the new You want me to wear?*

I often find myself frustrated with the dated parts of my home and my unkempt closets, imagining my friend's updated floor plan and organizing system. Without a minute or five to consider what's leading to my grumpiness after we gather in her home and I catch a glimpse of that closet, I'm spending my Saturday cleaning closets and tearing pictures out of the Restoration Hardware catalog for a dream board.

But with those three or five minutes and a quiet space and some practice at looking a little bit deeper, I see that I feel overwhelmed with our chaos and wishful that I could return to days when decorating could be a priority.

I have something to put off.

And I have something to put on.

But it's not about setting aside a beer can for sparkling water (or even the Restoration Hardware catalog for my Bible). It's about what's on the inside.

Recently I heard a woman described as "impressive." She could lead a room. She had a quick wit and sharp intelligence. In her young life, she had accomplished much and seemed to continue accomplishing much. She worked late into the night and won the attention of clients and prospective clients because of her willingness to go the extra mile, no matter the cost. More than that, she loved God and prayed with power.

But I'd seen behind the scenes. I'd seen the dark circles under her eyes and her nervous habits. I knew she felt frayed as a mom, not enough as a wife, a failure as a friend. She wasn't pleased with the work that wowed others.

She had a remarkable exterior life, but her inner life appeared to be headed for burnout. Christians around her applauded her diligence and her fervency in prayer, but they failed to notice the tightness in her gait.

We are often weak observers, of both ourselves and others, measuring the external and not looking beneath the surface. But the more I strengthen the skill of observing myself, the more I can see my neighbor. There are stories underneath our skin.

Most of us are not merely ignorant of them, we're scared to see them. We're afraid to look.

Seeing the stories beneath our skin can start as small as building moments into the day when we notice ourselves and our reactions to the world around us. Simple questions draw our attention to our interior lives, which crave God but often don't know how to access Him. They draw our attention to the stuck parts of ourselves.

How did I feel after that conversation?

What made my heart race today? And what did that heart-racing tell me about myself?

When did the fog set in and I was merely reacting and not present? What happened just before this fog that might have made my brain go offline?

Underneath my mad, was there sad?

At what point did I start to feel bad about myself?

What couldn't I erase from my mind?

What happened in my body and my thoughts after that conversation?

The pages of the Word tell us that God delights in truth in the inward being and teaches wisdom in the secret heart (Ps. 51:6).

God cares about these deeper parts of ourselves that the questions uncover. He made space inside us to implant wisdom in, but when we're mostly reacting, that secret heart from Psalm 51:6 is buried. Paying attention to what He cares about—the inner workings of our hearts—is a gentle process of excavating. We can't know the anxieties and the fears to bring to God unless we first notice them.

Our response to our limits is worth our attention.

The Word is full of God's care for the intricacies of the human heart, that heart we often ignore and shame with phrases like "Why can't I just get over this? I don't know why it feels so hard." He understands the intricacies of our hearts, but we have to first notice them before we can ask Him for that understanding. The psalmist said, "But when I thought how to understand this, it seemed to me a wearisome task, until I went into the sanctuary of God; then I discerned their end" (Ps. 73:16–17 ESV).

God gives discernment to those who ask for it, but we must pay attention to know how to ask.

Seeing the larger story that often predates the current circumstance gives us the ability to both have and hold context for an individual moment (and our response to it) and to grow through a limit that feels terribly restrictive. Here's what it looked like for me recently.

Nate got sick three days before I was scheduled to take a much needed retreat.

He rarely gets sick, so I was unpracticed in how to tend to him as well as the others (not to mention I was supposed to be packing). I puttered through the house somewhat aimlessly, as if I'd never had a sick spouse or a sick child before, leaving dishes in the laundry room as I stopped to change the laundry and forgetting to let the puppy out and staring into space as my teenagers asked for my attention. Even unthinking tasks required an unusual amount of effort. Preparing dinner and paying bills and filling out paperwork were impossible.

I recognize mindlessness as a clue for my heart that reads, *She's occupied with who knows what but is unmoving.* I spent a day or two in this state, merely responding—not considering the larger context for this moment, just reacting. More water for Nate, more supplements for the others so they don't get sick, change the babe's diaper, repeat.

Once Nate felt a bit better, I realized I'd befriended that old buddy dread. It's as familiar as the neighbor with whom you share a side yard—always present, a fixture in the landscape of your life.

Dread can steal my minutes (and my ability to imagine and dream and connect with the larger story of my life) like nothing else, yet I don't always notice it. It morphs me into someone who feels the need to be prepared for every scenario or brace her heart against expectations, but underneath both of those things is the foreboding sense that goodwill, again, evades me.

So you can see, I fell down a rabbit hole in my response to my limitations. Nate's sickness—my limitation at the moment—enabled an emotion to surface that long predated that particular bout with the flu. This was a moment not to miss but to notice, because what lay underneath could give me what my heart thirsts for most: deeper engagement with God.

As we grow in awareness of ourselves, things like dread come to light. We see context for a moment, and the emotion we're bringing (or not bringing) to that moment in light of our histories, and dread can lose its power. The rudders inside of us—the secret ones, the hidden navigators—lose strength when we see them for what they are and where they land within our stories and name them. They lose muscle when we talk to God about them.

Three days later, I sat on a loud plane and got quiet inside. Dread had its sway, but its power felt lesser, and it took only days, not weeks or months, to recognize it. Dread did not derail me. I felt it lurking, sure, but I had a name for it, and also a path carved around it. I recognized it as a snare, and I was able to slide along my hidden path instead of getting mired in the thicket.

When we name the emotions we've spent a lifetime avoiding, we let God shine a light into a well-established cobwebbed corner of our hearts, but one that doesn't always need to be there. Oh, the refreshment that light brings.

"We can . . . view our emotions from the perspective of whether they lead us to engagement with God or move us away from greater dependence on Him," write Dan Allender and Tremper Longman.[2]

It starts smaller than we think.

I pause and notice what my blustering days, my information-filled hours, my task-oriented ways all work to have me ignore: my larger story and God's work within it, before this moment and after it.

That's all.

I notice me. And Him, here.

But we often skip this critical life-and-daily step: paying attention.

This paying attention—being aware of what's churning inside of us—will look different in each person and has looked different for me in various stretches of my life.

For a long time, paying attention was a scheduled pause to hide away in the laundry room or my closet—somewhere no one would find me—to ask questions of my heart and trace the heart-racing and fingernail-biting back for some clue as to the source of this newly named anxiety.

In other seasons, it was one designated time a day when I got out in nature and read poetry and slowed my breathing to notice what won't stay buried in the fresh air and within wonder-filled moments.

Practicing the daily office several times a day is a recent habit of mine. Life looks different now than it did even five years ago: my teenagers' days are longer, my babies are now unstopping toddlers,

---

2. Dan B. Allender and Tremper Longman III, *The Cry of the Soul: How Our Emotions Reveal Our Deepest Questions about God* (Colorado Springs: NavPress, 2015), 26.

and I'm hungrier than ever for regular moments to check in with myself and heed God's still, small voice.

My strategy for noticing what I might bury can change in a heartbeat. Monday morning, I need instrumental worship music and a box of tissues. Tuesday, a few extra minutes with my journal in the afternoon, following the rabbit trail from my racing heart back to its anxious source. And Wednesday morning, this:

It's early morning and dark. I wake up in a malaise. Sleep hasn't erased yesterday's ache, it merely lies dormant. *There you are, again,* I think, reminded that the older I get, the less I can escape the things I'd like to forget.

I walk barefoot into the kitchen. My arms are heavy as I pour Nate's coffee to let it cool before he stumbles in after me ten minutes from now.

I sit down with my Bible and journal, unthinking. These morning rhythms are like a metronome—*tick, tick, tick*. I move through them, but my heart doesn't budge. It's stuck in yesterday and the swirl of that challenging relationship, the one that I fell asleep thinking about and woke up into. The one that, for all of Nate's holding and hand-holding, I can't seem to find comfort for. The one that, on more challenging days, makes me squirrely before God.

This morning I can't access vulnerability before God. I'm stuck. I don't know quite yet how to talk to God from this kind of ache. I just know that yesterday's pain throbs this morning, but I am still without words for it and, thus, without prayer for it.

I keep reading. Psalm 18, line by line, has become an old friend, as evidenced by the tear stains on the page. I'm not crying today, though. I'm numb.

I watch the clock, like most mornings—except most mornings, I wish time would slow, loving the dark cover that fall and winter mornings bring, receiving a brush with God that I know will sustain me. Today, though, I'm counting toward 7:10, or maybe even 7:00, when I can lose myself in the motion of the day and pretend the pain is not there. Should I go for a run today? It's not usually a question, but moping sounds like relief right now.

I let muscle memory take over, and I dress for the road. I won't talk myself out of this run if I can walk out the front door fast enough.

As is my practice, I run the first half mile in silence. It stretches into a mile. Before I know it, I've forgotten to turn on music or a podcast, lost in my thoughts again. I reach the mile-and-a-half marker, duck under the gate and into the secluded path through the woods, the one with little evidence of any other footsteps, the one I call mine.

Ahh. I catch my breath. The colors are brilliant back here, with no eyes but mine to see: golden bursts interrupted by burnt orange and some evergreen; reds clinging to the treetops, not giving in just yet.

I feel the lump in my throat.

I *feel*.

The numbness wears thin. Oh, *there's* my heart. (I finally notice it.) I swallow tears. God is here. God is with me. I forgot Him, but He didn't forget me. I see this in the way the light splinters through the trees and the branches that hang low, exposing the variegated field and forest beyond. The eastern bluebird, perched and hiding, is brilliant. God knows I love the details, and He shows Himself to me through them, right now. I can also see my heart with this adjusted lens—at least a little bit. And then I notice Him noticing me.

I reach two miles and turn back, my heart beating fast for more reasons than just the run. I hear the leaves underneath my feet, reminders of the death of summer. Change is coming. But the colorshow in front of my eyes speaks of life, beauty, and promise.

I'm alone in the woods, but I'm not alone. God carries me. He pursues me.

My heart pounds and sweat trickles down the sides of my face. This isn't mere exercise. I'm reviving. Revival requires being present—mentally, physically, and emotionally—all things that I couldn't access before I laced my shoes and walked out the front door.

I've been a runner for thirty-two years, but I discovered only recently how running helps me pay attention. Some days we need to move out of our heady experience of God and know Him as the embodied one who also embodies us with His Spirit. I need to hear my feet pounding pavement or crunching leaves to feel my heart reverberating. I need to slow enough to notice myself in the world—leaving tracks on the dusty trail and making deer scatter and running through a lump in my throat that didn't surface until I started moving—to then see God in my world.

Self-awareness can lead to God-awareness if we let it. Being aware of ourselves can start as small and as simple as noticing our heart rate racing on a long day, telling us the story of anxiety we hadn't seen, fear that needs His attention. It can be as simple as noticing how my pent-up emotions need the release that comes when my feet crush leaves underneath me and I find my heart inside me.

We can't receive the story God has for us—the story He has written, a love letter chicken-scratched on the fence, meeting us where we are—if we don't first notice how we relate to that fence.

―――― *For Your Continued Pursuit* ――――

Psalm 34:5 | Psalm 51:6 | Psalm 73:16–17 | Psalm 119:73 | Psalm 119:105 | Psalm 139:23–24 | Hosea 2:6 | John 4:13–14 | Ephesians 4:22–24 | Philippians 3:20 | 1 John 1:5

9

SLOWER STILL

Embracing the Fence Line

Beyond morass and mountains swells the star.
—George MacDonald, *Diary of an Old Soul*

The December of my senior year of college, my parents' landline rang at one thirty in the morning. My mom stumbled into my room and handed me the phone as a hysterical teenager cried on the other end: "She's dead, Sara. She's dead."

I had just arrived home from college for winter break. I clutched the phone while trying to orient myself in the face of sudden tragedy. My mom was in her nightgown beside me. *I'm not on East Vine Street in Oxford, Ohio.* I sat up and put my feet on the carpeted floor. *I'm not sleeping in the house with old wood floors that I share with my housemates.* Slowly I revived to my surroundings and this terrible news all at the same time: one of the high school students I mentored through our college ministry had just died. She was hit by a car while her best friend witnessed it, and that's who was calling me from the police station.

Renee's death was the first time I experienced the abrupt loss of someone that felt out of time. Though she was only four years younger than me, she is now forever young, still sixteen in my mind. I told her about Jesus and read the Bible with her, intermixed with conversations about boys, crushes, and eye shadow. We went to a swim meet together the day before she died. Of course, neither of us knew that the swim meet was our goodbye.

In the months that followed—the last four months of my senior year of college—I couldn't keep pace as I had during the previous three-and-a-half years. I'd so nimbly juggled relationships with my roommates, college classes, and my ministry to high school students, but now everything felt like work those last few months of school. My muscles and my mind filled with what I called lethargy. Senioritis, perhaps. Not only had some of my joy in reaching high school students with the gospel been buried with Renee, so had my energy.

I dreamed about catching mono so I'd have an excuse to slow the pace I'd set for myself in my first three years of college. (Apparently, grief wasn't enough of a reason to take a pause.) Instead, I did what I knew best: I kept forging ahead like a good little soldier, doing my work for the kingdom and ignoring my heart and my body to do so.

I crawled across the finish line—walked the stage for my honors diploma, had countless goodbye dinners with other high school students in whom I'd invested, and went on a week's vacation to the beach, assuming it was the recharge I needed to remember my vision and focus and get back in the game.

We didn't use words like *burnout* then, or if we did use them, they felt like excuses for people who couldn't keep pace. So I topped off at the beach and kept running until I couldn't anymore, until my legs said no more. My body knew the motions, but somewhere inside that summer my heart ran out of fuel.

Many of us run through the warning signals from our hearts, heads, friends, church leaders, and spouses until our legs say no more. Rather than scolding ourselves for not heeding all the signs, perhaps we need to look kindly upon our bodies, which will tell us what our hearts and minds can't receive. These physical pains are a gift. Sore muscles tell me I need to jog or walk on my next run. Neck pain reminds me to take a break from the screen. Swollen glands in my neck urge me to drink more water, take vitamin C, and sleep longer than usual.

My body is a gift. It talks to me even when I've silenced my heart.

I resent it when my body slows me, but the God who was also man wore the same frame and didn't. We race and pace ourselves as limitless ones, but Jesus let His body drift to sleep in a boat during a rising storm.

After years of praying for my migraines to end, I wondered whether they were telling me something. For years I prayed simple, prayers of supplication—*Jesus, heal my head; Jesus, lift this ache*—before even thinking that these headaches might be cries for attention.

Our bodies tell us stories when we let them, especially if we're unwilling to notice our hearts. Sometimes that story from God is simple: *slower still.*

One Wednesday morning, before the sun rose, I woke to a cocktail of a headache, body aches, fever, and nausea. Nate was states away at a conference. God had two hours to answer my prayer to heal me before the little girls started their morning pillow fights and the teenagers started rummaging through the fridge for breakfast and my closet for clothes. So I prayed, *Jesus, bring relief to my body*—a prayer I've known and from which I have experienced fruit and healing.

But I also know the power of *not yet*, and this particular morning, I suspected He had a story for me within my skin.

Seven thirty came, and my symptoms worsened. The younger version of myself would have wondered why God tarried and why me. But the forty-five-year-old version knew: He had something for me today. I commissioned the teenagers as babysitters and pulled the covers over my head, interrupted only occasionally by shouts outside the bedroom door that sometimes indicated that all was well, and sometimes that chaos was in charge. I was too sick to pay attention.

Hours later, I padded out of the bedroom to find the remains of crafts, art projects, and snacks, all tools to occupy fidgety little ones. Though now the house was quiet. My oldest had taken the younger ones to a park, and the teenagers were in class. Only the dog and I shared these acres of quiet.

I couldn't remember the last time I'd been in our home quiet and alone. Sure, I'd shared the space with sleeping people, but something about having the whole house to myself was deeply settling. As I waited for the little ones to return, my body restored. I felt alert and expectant.

I read a novel and prayed intermittently—the kind of puttering prayer I used to engage in more readily when I didn't have so many people in my home. I watched autumn from my window.

Slower still dropped into my mind as if it were a whisper from God. We were in a stretch where life felt unusually fast-paced for us, but with elements we could never quite slow. Bath times, dinner for nine, and coordinating cars for working teenagers aren't easily purged from a schedule. My body was exhausted from it all.

As I absorbed that phrase, I realized it was congruent with what I'd been reading in my Bible in the dark of the morning and sensing as I prayed before little people made my world loud. I had not done much with what I'd read or perceived—not until this morning when the deep fatigue of body aches and drooping eyelids and a pounding headache gave me no option but to slow.

This is often how He works, using our skin as the fence line, saying with action more than words *slower still* to a society of people who can't calculate the cost of their pace.

If not our skin, then our schedules, our pocketbooks, or our friend groups shift—He pares back when we cannot. He gently leads, as if we're still schoolgirls and schoolboys needing to be told when it's time for recess and time for reading.

I remember the black-tie wedding where I wore what I could find in my closet because our finances were too tight to purchase something new. And the critical court date for a friend that Nate attended without me because we had no babysitters to watch our crew at home. And the babies who didn't get an alert mommy or the teenagers who didn't get an attentive mom because she was stretched at both ends of the day.

He pared and pruned.

I wasn't there the morning my dad died, and I didn't attend my nephew's graduation. I missed a dear friend's daughter's wedding as I labored to bring my daughter Virginia into the world.

Slower still is the invitation for our finances and friendships and our mothering and fathering when what we have cannot stretch over what we perceive is needed. *Slower still* is not the consolation prize for those without faith that God will heal, increase, or change our circumstances. It is the gift.

"To make prayer your life priority," wrote J. I. Packer, "as countless Christians of former days did outside as well as inside the monastery, is stupendously difficult in a world that runs you off your feet and will not let you slow down."[1] Talking to God can be impossible with the current of our lives. And yet that connection is what our hearts most crave.

Slower still comes to you and me in the form of things we might otherwise see as fences. *Slower still*, as we embrace the "come, die, grieve, live" cycle that God gives us, can become the words we use to lead us before our bodies do. Come (choose to step forward and not stay stuck), die (let Him have His way with us), grieve (collapse into God and remember, in our collapsing, that our longings matter), and live (truly live)—and *slower still* as we go.

One morning, as Nate and I had our daily thirty-minute coffee "date" before he left for work, Charlotte climbed over my ankles and into his lap. "I love you, Daddy . . . so much. Snuggle me?" She tucked her head under his neck, sucked her thumb, and closed her eyes—for fifteen seconds. Then she shimmied off his lap and began humming *Pomp and Circumstance*. "Charlotte! Jane! Hagerty!" She recited her name, with an emphasis on each part, just as she'd heard the week before at her sister's graduation. "Wooo!" She added the applause. For days, she'd been "practicing graduation," cap and all.

I found out I was pregnant with Charlotte at one of the lowest points of our married lives—low not in our marriage but with our family. I was forty-two but felt like I was about eighty. My body was

---

1. Tim Keller, *First John Leader's Guide* (New York: Redeemer Presbyterian Church, 2007), 4.

not taking well to a fourth pregnancy at this age. Our big kids were fielding some of the worst pains of their early childhood trauma for the first time, and at the same time. I couldn't believe God would add more cargo to this sinking ship.

For six months, I let myself wrestle. I knew it didn't scare God for me to wrestle. Well-intentioned friends and acquaintances assured me that God wouldn't give me more than I could handle, but I poked holes in this theory in my private conversations with Him. It wasn't until July—a few months before Charlotte's October due date—that I finally had the earliest inkling that one more child might not sink our ship. That she might give us wings.

She came on a snowy October morning. It's the only October snow I remember from our thirteen years in Kansas City. After a surprisingly challenging labor, I held her with the whispers of winter outside my window but knew it was spring for us.

With Charlotte came laughter again.

Was it possible that another child made life lighter than it had been, not heavier? Sure, some more diapers and night feedings felt out of time for me and Nate in our midlife, but something shifted in our home with this baby who I'd been sure would sink us.

She formed bonds with my big kids who needed a greater attachment to our home and family. She made us simplify: after months of pouring time, money, and energy into treatments for the healing of trauma, we had to slow our pace, and we found a God who didn't withhold when we weren't at one hundred percent.

Charlotte is one of the hundreds of stories in my adult life of when God did the opposite of what I expected. She entered my scrapbook of "exceedingly abundantly above all that we ask or think" (Eph. 3:20 NKJV). And that scrapbook gets thicker with the years.

Telling and retelling myself the stories of God in and through my weakness shapes how I respond to ever-growing weakness, to the *slower still* invitations that come near daily, when the inertia of my life butts into God's pace for me.

"We must be ready to allow ourselves to be interrupted by God," said Dietrich Bonhoeffer. "God will be constantly crossing our paths and canceling our plans."[2] And oftentimes, that interruption comes in weakness. Snow days and sickness and broken ankles and unexpected pregnancies and canceled flights and barren wombs—God slows us when we cannot slow ourselves.

The real part of partnering with Him is when we choose to make steps toward slowing ourselves, toward finding the boundaries and thriving within them, even before we have an injury.

We're raised, even within Christianity at times, on a diet of *I can do anything*, but we follow a God who slept.

We cherry-pick portions of Scripture that lead us to push every limit and challenge every boundary, and yet Jesus wearied.

He came bound by skin, too. Perhaps our understanding of His limitlessness and the limitlessness we have in Him needs to start with understanding our likeness.

George MacDonald said, "Freedom is to be like thee, face and heart. To know it, Lord, I must be as thou art."[3] So we look small and live small and seek to move slowly not for its own sake but as an attempt to let our humanity boundary us. And from that place—that small, boundaried place—comes grandeur.

---

2. Dietrich Bonhoeffer, *Life Together* (San Francisco: HarperSanFrancisco, 1954), 99.

3. George MacDonald, *Diary of an Old Soul* (Mansfield Centre, CT: Martino Publishing, 2015), May 28.

Choosing slow requires not only the mental decision but also the daily outworking.

Several years ago, I rocked a newborn babe for hours a day and realized in the forced slow of the infant months that there were elements of my day and life that were untouchable—not on the table for discussion—but were weighing on me. I eked productivity out of after-bedtime hours and the minutes between my morning quiet and when alarms went off in the upstairs bedrooms. I squeezed minutes of responding to emails and texts, ordering household supplies, and scheduling dentist appointments as the children took extra time to lace their shoes. Even while the youngest one was buckled into his car seat, I discovered I could steal time. I was a master tasker; I had to be, I reasoned. How else can one endure such responsibility as having this many children? (I'd forgotten that this habit started long before kids.) I prided myself on multitasking.

So as this round-faced babe kept me for long hours in a chair—rocking her, holding her, studying the folds of flesh around her wrists and her tiny eyelashes and fingertips—I realized that what I once deemed admirable possibly was not. I thought I was stealing minutes from a finite day when I quickly responded to an email or ordered more batteries online, but the slowness of the rocking chair made me wonder whether the minutes were, instead, being stolen from me.

I observed winter that winter. I didn't just freeze underneath it. I remember absorbing the blanketing of the snow and the power of quiet as the woods hushed underneath it. I associate this sweet babe's early days with pajamas and tea and tearful conversations with God about things that surface only when our heart rates slow enough to hear what's underneath them.

She was my quietest baby—mostly content, mostly happy being held. I still wonder whether it's because those were some of my most tranquil days. Sure, chaos happened outside the bedroom where I rocked her, hour after hour, but it was the chaos of squabbling siblings and fort-building and dishes clattering in the kitchen as kids climbed on the countertops to add to the stack. It was the normal noise of life, not the internal noise I create with my flurry to saute onions, listen to a podcast, and respond to three texts, all simultaneously.

Winter was still, and so was I, still enough that I chose to let the stillness seep into spring. I didn't know how to slow life without a baby requiring that slowness. As she learned to crawl, babble, and sleep on her own, I knew I needed to find a stillness outside this baby, my pacer.

So I created an experiment for myself: the productivity fast. I knew it wasn't a lifetime experiment but a laboratory. I wondered: if I "fasted" from what I thought was one of my greatest gifts, what might my life look like? How would I feel about God? How would I feel about myself? How would I think God felt about me?

I pared my list of tasks by seeing myself as a mother of a newborn, capable of not much more than sustaining this life. Instead of putting six things on my list for the day, I put two. Instead of making countless lists to be addressed after the list before them was completed, I limited my expectations of myself.

I let things go by putting them in ink—I didn't trust myself to scale down figuratively. I allowed my short list to dictate what I would do. When the list was over, I was done. And the list wasn't designed for the woman who is swift with time and skilled at multitasking. It was designed with skin in mind—His skin and mine.

I wanted to notice which of the trees I'd seen for years from my back porch bloomed first in spring. Where did the robins lay their eggs? Where did the hummingbirds return, day after day? When did the bunnies come out of hibernation and find their way back into our yard?

And that spring, I felt the grass between my toes, made bud vases of dogwood clippings, and watched my daughter's growth in days, not years or even months. Less productive, more present. Less accomplished, more alive. Less masterful, more peaceful.

And the short list never meant we went without groceries or dinner. We paid our taxes and got oil changes, all of the children were dutifully shuttled to their activities, and I got pulled over only once for an expired registration.

Somehow the important things happened, and when they didn't, we all survived. And with each item missed, something inside me grew stronger, more resolute, as if to say with my life and my days, "And my God will supply every need of yours" (Phil. 4:19 ESV).

The less productive I was, the fuller my life became. Sure, I was skittish, some days enjoying the fruit of not living a productivity-driven life, and others wondering who I was without my tasks. But I needed this experiment to prove to myself what the years had been whispering to me: life is not found when you think you have it all. More is less, in His way. Less is more.

I lost my long lists and multitasking, but I inched toward a softer, more receptive connection with God.

I can't look at the strands on the top of Bo's head without thinking of when I learned how his hair turns to gold at just the right angle in the sunlight. I missed this when my task list was my goal.

Nate, too, made these choices in his way.

One weekend when he met with other business owners and leaders in their field, he shared the reality of his days. Life with so many children and the surprising needs that often come when you're raising children who have experienced trauma meant that his nine-to-five usually had to be much less than nine to five. He didn't stumble in late and bolt from his desk early; he chose to trim what would have been a significant investment in his business so that our home life could be more rhythmic, less chaotic, even amid the natural chaos that comes with our mix.

This was vulnerable for him to share among men and women who watched the clock not for dinner but for eking productivity out of every minute, unfettered in their businesses. Who wouldn't applaud overtime and overinvestment in the name of growth?

Sharing in that circle made him acutely aware of the consequences of his choice of *slower still*. Less revenue, growth, and opportunity came with fewer work hours, less travel, and less time for connections.

But did it?

We took the pause and considered the financial *and* emotional fruit in his business since his company began instituting a sabbatical rhythm. (They work a seven-week push, then take the eighth week off to rest and reset.) It didn't match up—as we often see when we lean into the boundaries of our human limitations. More significant than that, though, was the fruit in his heart.

My man is growing in understanding of his weakness, a soft skill that's required for men shedding their boyhoods but often is undervalued in the world of speed. His love for Jesus and understanding of Jesus' love for him is growing in step with the gray spreading across his beard and hair. He wakes up craving the Word (and his coffee). These later, slower days are producing depths inside him that fast-paced Nate never knew.

We both are shedding our high expectations of ourselves and

finding God, as we are becoming more comfortable with earning a B-minus at the things that are most valuable in life and focusing on our heart-connect with Him.

In Matthew 11:28–30, Jesus says, "Come to Me, all you who labor and are heavy laden, and I will give you rest. Take My yoke upon you, and learn from Me, for I am gentle and lowly in heart, and you will find rest for your souls. For My yoke is easy, and My burden is light" (NKJV).

Tired is a gift. We don't know rest until we lean into the weariness of our labor. It reveals the limits of our skin and our time and our energies, the limits that teach us to lean into a God who shares of Himself with the ones He chose to encase in flesh.

Tired is a gift.

There are many more ways to lean into our limits and facilitate the "come, die, grieve, live" cycle in our lives. They are subtle, like choosing *not* to bring dinner to a friend in need at a time when our bodies and hearts can't swing it. Subtle, like saying no to a night out for a friend's birthday or holding a child back from another three-year-old's birthday party to keep life at home just a tad bit slower and more present. The nos that can feel the least "Christian"—the ones we tell ourselves are selfish and lazy—are often ones that form us into being listeners of God, not of our impulses.

A selected weekly sabbath and sabbaticals that are more than vacations but are intentional times of rest are other ways to lean into our limits. But first, we must address our unwillingness to go rest and consider what the stubborn refusals might be telling us of our hearts. "If we dig down a little deeper," Ruth Haley Barton writes, "we may see that our unwillingness to practice sabbath is really an unwillingness to live within the limits of our humanity, to honor our finiteness."[4]

Beyond every extra yes and *I can cram in one more email* is a story worth pursuing with God. *Why can't I say no here?* And as that conversation continues our ability to lean into, rather than push against, the limits He gives us will grow. And trust takes a deeper root.

Psalm 139:5 says, "You hem me in, behind and before, and lay your hand upon me" (ESV). *Hem* also can be translated as "beset." Oh, the ache of being hemmed, beset. The Hebrew equates this with "to confine, secure, shut in, enclose."

He builds a fence around us. We live it. We feel it.

And eventually, as we grow, we embrace it.

———— *For Your Continued Pursuit* ————

Psalm 119:96 | Psalm 139:5 | Proverbs 3:5–6 | Matthew 11:28–30 | John 4:5–6 | 1 Corinthians 1:25 | 2 Corinthians 12:9 | Ephesians 3:20–21 | Philippians 1:6 | Philippians 3:10 | Philippians 4:19

———

4. Ruth Haley Barton, *Sacred Rhythms: Arranging Our Lives for Spiritual Transformation* (Downers Grove, IL: InterVarsity Press, 2006), 138.

10

THE BETTER FOOD FOR OUR DISHEVELED HEADS

The Beginnings of Limitlessness, within Our Limits

> The ultimate freedom we have as human beings is the power to select what we will allow or require our minds to dwell upon. We are not totally free in this respect. But we do have great freedom here.
>
> —DALLAS WILLARD, RENOVATION OF THE HEART

IT'S EARLY.

The house is dark and quiet, and cold.

I shuffle to turn on the teapot and pour Nate's time-brewed coffee, still hazed with sleep. I'm tempted to do what draws us most easily in the unthinking minutes—to scroll, to feed the haze—but after pouring my tea, I sink into my morning chair, which sits in front of the one fire in this house that can start with a switch.

I'm grateful for that switch this morning—no blowing into tinder to grow a flame. I wrap myself in the thickest blanket we own. Sometimes I wonder whether it's the quiet, the dark, the uninterrupted morning with a warm cup of tea, more than Jesus and these ancient pages, that make me return each day. But I'm here and I'm a tangle of thoughts from yesterday, unfinished conversations, tasks that were finished and led to others, tasks that buzz in my ear like mosquitos. I don't come as a student, bright-eyed to learn with sharpened number-two pencils and a clean page. I come full. Filled up with murky thoughts and questions about life and my heart, and sometimes even just numbness—full of numbness.

But this is what I bring: me. I bring myself to the Word and to Jesus. Not a fantasy of what I think I should be as a "godly woman"—mother, wife, and friend. I bring my anxiety, fear, and dull approach to God. And we meet. And instead of my day starting as if the run-on sentence from the night before just needed a page-turn to continue, I have a reset. The reset often looks like an uncertain little girl (who wears the responsibilities of a grown woman on the other side of this bedroom door when the sun breaks the morning dark) bringing her squirmy soul to the one who can hold it.

So I crack open the Word, and it feels foreign to me.

Yes, I read it yesterday and probably even heard it at different points throughout my day. But this morning, it feels foreign—as cold as the air against my fingers or the wooden floor against my bare toes. Instead of bristling at how distant and disconnected from my reality the Word feels, I trust that I will acclimate to it if I stay. I know I will want more of it than the world wants of me. I'll warm to the gentle whispers of God, like breath on my neck. I'll unfurl a bit more into who I was made to be, not who I am working so hard to be to buoy myself in this torrent of a world—not in giant leaps but slowly and shuffling.

And it may be ninety percent me, all amuck with thoughts and anxiety swirls, and only ten percent His Word and His tender but assuring grip around me, but it's ten percent more than if I'd hurled myself out of bed and into the narrative of what the world wants of me, even the narrative of what I want of me.

These quiet, dark minutes are few, but they are essential for this day.

Of course, the warm tea, blanket, and fire help, but the magic is in being held. That little girl couldn't possibly do another day with any measure of success without knowing that she is held from the moment she wakes up.

For many years, I scolded myself into having what we once called "quiet times"—as if I could get on the nice (not naughty) list if I checked this box. And once I realized that this report card I'd made for myself was far from God's heart for me, I spent years trying to unlearn reaching for His approval with a quiet time and relearn how to approach His Word without that fictitious approval.

And I wonder now, a decade or so later, whether, back then, if I had been invited instead into the narrative of "come because your soul craves this, because your day will feel different (even if it doesn't look different) because of it, because this is the food your heart needs most," I might have seen it all differently. This habit of reading the Word each day, this morning time of being held doesn't change how He sees me, but it dramatically changes how I live and see the world.

For you, it might be the quiet of the night, when all the tasks are tucked away on your desk and all the little feet are tucked in their beds, that you can let yourself be held. Or it may be midafternoon, for ten minutes or less, when you hide in the corner of the house or the empty office in your building and set His Word onto your lap and yourself in His arms. The key isn't what I thought it was all those years ago: the format, the time, the effort. The key is bringing my unkempt heart into a place where His Word can hold me, where I can let myself be seen by Him, where I position myself to need Him and to receive what He has to say to my neediness.

Though this practice doesn't change how God sees me, it changes how I see God.

I can't deny that my days are growing progressively smoother, despite adding more children, experiencing more heartache, having more chaos in my life. The more I make it a practice to sit in His lap, with all the mess of me, the more settled I feel.

But it's a bit of a fight.

We wrestle with thoughts—experts say six thousand of them in a day. Many of them counter the truth of the Word—fears and anxieties and untruths seeking to direct our lives and often succeeding. It exhausts us.

From when my toes touch the morning-chilled floor until I fall into bed, I'm surrounded by thoughts, many that oppose God. Sometimes they tell me I'm invincible and need to overcome my limits. Other times they serve as report cards, measuring my progress. Still other times, they coach me to reach for what I don't have.

The Word is the counterbalance to these thoughts. But I have to engage with it.

Our daughter has always been a musician. Some of our first friends to visit her in the orphanage caught a ring of the music in her bones. That a crowd of her peers was watching didn't threaten her. She belted out a song in front of the other children at the orphanage.

And she came home with us singing.

A decade later, we flew her across the country for her thirteenth birthday to see her favorite musician perform. In an "only God" stroke (and through the introduction of a generous friend), we arranged for her to meet him before he went on stage. This unforgettable night was sandwiched between our typical nights of Nate schooling her in the history of music—sharing vignettes of his favorites, imparting discernment for sound and lyric, traveling through decades of song in fifteen-minute increments in the car and after dinner. Her dad, her sherpa through the world of music.

The day after we landed home from the concert, just before dinner, Nate said, "Sweet, it's time to shut down your music for dinner." In a flurry of emotion, she told me, "Dad's against my music!"

It would have been easy to write this off as an inconvenience, a tantrum, an outburst that didn't require much thought. On the contrary, though, this little moment told a story.

My little girl carried into our home years of negative understanding and experience about what a dad is and what a dad does. Before we adopted her, she'd lived within a painful narrative that didn't relent merely because she had a new father, name, and address. A decade later, she had a dad who invested in her heart, her passions, and her particular wiring—new whispers of tenderness, new attentiveness to her young heart, new shoulders for her to rest her head on—but still the old narrative trapped her.

We're not all that different from her.

Our relationship with the Word is complicated, just like my daughter's is with her dad. History, narrative, and hurt inform whether, in a moment of stress, I pick up that book and talk to the Man wrapped within it or instead read another news article and scroll through my feed.

We often toggle between shame for not reading the Word—perhaps saying "I'm giving myself grace" to evade the shame, rather than analyzing why we're avoiding it—and a false sense of strength when we've disciplined ourselves into picking it up. Though you might not experience either of these impulses, there are reasons we don't read our Bibles or receive the words as sterile and distant when we do. We have a complicated relationship with the Word and its author, but we make it simple: I'm just tired, I don't have time, and it doesn't inspire me the way some other author's writing does.

End of story.

Except that our oversimplified reasons for not picking up this Word, which is full of life for our needy times, parched hearts, and lost souls, prevent us from having the most important conversation of our lives: *God, why do You feel so distant? Why am I choosing this world's inspirational words over Yours? Why don't I want to scoot up next to You? Why does this Word, which is You, feel sterile to me?*

You might even come up with a response like my girl's "Dad's against my music," one that needs a little more unpacking, a lot more tender unraveling, a gentle understanding from Him.

Instead of berating ourselves into better Bible reading habits or feeling spurts of false strength when we've "followed the plan" on our best days, maybe we need to face Him.

Face the Word that we either left dusty or approached at a theological distance, and ask questions of our hearts: *How did I get here, not seeing a person behind the Word? Is there a part of my history when I received fear or shame related to Scripture that makes this Word feel less than life to me? What happens in my interior life as I pick up this book?*

Because this Man inside the Word is living. Active in our lives. Closer than skin. Tender with our failings. Gentle. Present to lead us, and exactly how we need to be led.

Even the best sermon, book, or podcast is not enough to give us what we need for the days ahead, not even enough to buoy us for more than a few weeks or days. His Word, however, can change us.

It can change how we see the fence line. It can reach into us, disrupt old thought patterns, and reshape the way we think, see, and engage with the world around us.

If we can consider the obstacles to getting us there, with His Word in our laps or mouths, we might stand a fighting chance in this tug-of-war of our minds.

I have started to scan the landscape for the woman I want to be in ten and fifteen and twenty years. Observing in church settings and retreats and even on my street the women who have a life I want, what do they have in common?

They don't all have the family of my dreams or even the job I want. They don't all have homes I could find myself calling home or live in areas of the country where I'd like to live. They don't all have the trendiness or youthfulness I hope to hold. What each of them has is a settledness about them. A peace. A lack of striving, pushing to make things happen. An ability to stay present. They like where they are, even if they don't love the stories they have had to endure.

Psalm 16:5–6 says, "The LORD is my chosen portion and my cup; you hold my lot. The lines have fallen for me in pleasant places; indeed, I have a beautiful inheritance" (ESV). Line this up against the first thought you had this morning or what went through your mind when something unexpected happened this week or your observations of the painful or nagging situation that hangs like a low cloud over even your best Christmas-morning days. The difference is stark.

Because most of us don't have the ongoing, daily experience of the Word changing our thoughts, we distance ourselves from it emotionally. We become like visitors to a museum or an art exhibit.

We marvel at the layers and texture and light. When we see beauty, we picture what that might look like in our foyers or family rooms or over our beds. We dream about buying such pieces, and then we go home.

But if we can notice the historical hurdles that keep us from climbing into the painting and experiencing the light as it dances on what was once still, we can dialogue with God through it.

If we talk to God through His Word and from our pain over our limitations, the Word moves from the didactic, which can shift the mind for a bit but rarely changes a heart, to the personal.

Dallas Willard writes, "Spiritual formation in Christ . . . [is a] total interchange of our ideas and images for his."[1]

This interchange must start somewhere. And often, it starts very small. Who I want to be in ten or twenty years starts with one minute.

Imagine this day. You wake up to this thought: *I have a good thing going, my limitations are needed and purposed, I have a beautiful, beautiful house of life.*

What would six in the morning feel like if you woke into that thought? What if you received it in your person as you fielded the terse comment from a friend, the news on your phone, or another surprise bill from your doctor?

It's seven thirty in the morning, a time typically loud and disruptive to my quiet, but I'm tucked away in a hotel room on the Kansas City Plaza on my quarterly getaway. Outside my window, the traffic

---

1. Dallas Willard, *Renovation of the Heart: Putting on the Character of Christ* (Colorado Springs: NavPress, 2002), 102.

has picked up, the lights are on in the office buildings surrounding the strip of high-end stores and quaint boutiques, and people are filing in to their jobs, coffee in hand and toothpaste probably still fresh on their breaths. The temperatures have dropped below freezing, and the roses in the rose garden just over the hill have dropped their blooms. Life and winter plunder beauty, or so I think as I hug myself under the blanket I brought from home, anticipating this cold.

Those people outside my window are moving through their day, many mechanically, but I have scheduled a pause to watch them as if I'm watching myself. I don't drink coffee or have a commute to work, but seven thirty is in my muscle memory. They are limited by their punch cards and all-staff meetings, by having to be on time, driving quickly past the seventy-five-acre park half a mile from this hotel. I am limited by dirty diapers and teenagers asking how to format their essays in MLA an hour before they're due. All of us would probably like a long walk around that park.

But would we take it?

I can step through the foyer of this hotel and run for a quarter of a mile to get to that seventy-five-acre park and its pond, fountain, and rose garden, its mature trees and long stretches of grass and, in summer, dozens of varieties of roses circling the center. And while you might say you'd choose that walk, any day, over clocking in at a retail store or preparing PowerPoint presentations, and I might say I'd prefer that walk over fixing meals for finicky eaters and running another load of laundry, we both might choose otherwise in actuality.

These are the daily choices.

The inertia of my life pulls me toward flurry, reactivity, busyness. But there's a whisper in the back of my mind, a calloused hand on my shoulder reminding me that there's another way to live with the same schedule and the same amount of laundry and the same responsibilities.

I have tried it before, this one choice. It's the daily practice of adoration, talking to God from His Word, right where I am. I've written about it and lived it for a decade, and yet I still need to be reminded: *Choose to adore and you will see fruit.*

So this morning, even though my usual limitations aren't bearing down on me, I'm going to choose this other way because something inside reminds me that choices here and there—minute-sized choices—eventually lead to a lifestyle, a way of being.

The rose garden is accessible, yes, even in the retail store.

And here's what it looks like:

This morning, my heart feels cold and distant, just like the wintered plaza. I'm tired of being tired. Some of the needs in our home have been especially loud as of late—and messy. The mess feels weighty, uncalculated, without an expiration date. So to be honest, I'd like to choose to be grumpy about what limits me in my home and family rather than be coerced into having thoughts that could unbind me.

I have had enough experience with this little practice I call adoration to know that what feels good for a moment—nurturing resentment and a chilled heart, or avoiding it all and giving in to numbness—doesn't compare to when my heart gets lifted by His Word.

This is what it looks like for me. I open my Bible to the Psalms:

> The LORD preserves the simple;
>> when I was brought low, he saved me.
> Return, O my soul, to your rest;
>> for the LORD has dealt bountifully with you.

For you have delivered my soul from death,
   my eyes from tears,
   my feet from stumbling.

—PSALM 116:6–8 ESV

This morning, I'm like a visitor at a museum again. *Oh! Isn't that beautiful?* I stand distant and observing, not letting this Word come close, because I'm too unfamiliar with what's inside of me to invite someone else into it. I want just to visit and go home.

Realizing that to step into this painting—to see the colors through my own eyes and experience the light splintering—I best start with me if I can't start with Him. So I pray from the real, the raw, even though I feel rusty doing so: *God, I am brought low. My heart feels heavy. My life feels too much but not enough. There is no rest here, only unsettledness.*

I sit long enough to feel what I've just named and to name, again, what I start to feel. This is the early inkling of a conversation with God.

Then I move from His Word, from the didactic, into my own words: *Your Word tells me that You save me here. I don't feel like I could possibly be saved from this stuckness, but I am asking, Would You meet me, and would You save me? Oh, I adore You, God who saves, even when I feel like I'm too lost to be saved.*

I sit again, in silence, this time absorbing His Word, not just reading it. Uncorking my thoughts and naming them gives me the ability to receive.

I adore You, God, that You deliver—my soul from this daily death, my eyes from the tears of years, my feet from their ever-always stumbling. I adore You that there is bounty for me, a bountiful life, even though it feels terribly limited at the moment.

I let those words hang in the air. I consider them. I consider myself. I consider Him intersecting my inner life. I'm not turning on my heel, away from the painting, settling into being an observer as my Christian practice. Instead, I'm letting the discomfort of my thoughts and my heart invite me to step into the beauty.

Now, this is a truncated version of what sometimes spans an hour and sometimes gets condensed into the three minutes I have as I move the laundry from the washer to the dryer. This is adoration: the nexus of my vulnerable thoughts, exposed by His Word, where His Word doesn't just teach my thoughts but encircles them.

This engagement with the Word is not flashy or grandiose, but it can penetrate the soul the way His Word is intended to do if we let it. I can't see my limits as anything other than what the six thousand thoughts a day are telling me, unconsciously, unless I challenge them gently with His Word, inviting the lurkers in my mind to come out into the light and be held and then released so His Word can take its place.

One of those six thousand thoughts this morning, gently released and replaced. Another this afternoon. Three tomorrow. God's pace is often much slower than we'd like, but it's gentle and kind, and over time, if we participate, our minds change.

We consider capacity as a sum-total pie. I have eight slices to give and can give only eight. If I give away seven, I have only one left. So if I have twenty-four hours in a day and can live only sixteen of them, at best, I can parcel them out according to what needs are most present—mine and my children's and Nate's—but still I have only sixteen to give. (Well, maybe a few extra if the toddler wakes in the night.) We treat our capacity as finite, but when we consider the six thousand thoughts that occupy our lives—our minutes, our seconds—our apparent capacity involves more than the hours we have to work with in a day.

Last spring, I received information that sent me into fear and dread in a flash of a second. My mind went offline. I might as well have been drooling. I missed the three main items for which I went to Costco. I couldn't remember the route I drove home. I saw my children's mouths moving but heard no sound. I cooked dinner and bought eyeglasses and read stories to eager toddlers, all while my mind traveled elsewhere.

My mind drove me that day. I was merely a passenger on the train of my thoughts, destined for nowhere.

Many days our minds drive us without our agreement or even awareness.

We assess situations, make decisions, interact with friends, and field news, mostly unthinkingly. Except, we're always thinking.

Always thinking.

There is a world between my two ears that informs how I see my children, what I notice about Nate, how I react to a neighbor's complaint or a friend's throwaway comment or a thread I read online. Six thousand thoughts per day pass through my mind, yet when I feel overwhelmed, I run to tweak my schedule or attempt to duck a paralyzing situation. I ignore that my sense of overwhelm may come from within my thoughts rather than my circumstances.

We have a million tools at our disposal to improve and maximize our output. We can manage the minutiae of our schedules and multitask for more minutes. We can say no to more things and yes to less. We can manage our time in minutes, not hours. All of these things are needed, but if our interior lives remain unexamined, we are redecorating a house that is burning to the ground.

My mind drives my day. And it defines my capacity. It defines how I live within the fence line.

Part of the "come, die, grieve, live" cycle includes the renewing of our minds. The more renewal I experience in the parts of my life that no one sees, the more my capacity grows. On many days with seven kids, I have a greater capacity to engage with what He's put in front of me than I did when I had two children and much less responsibility. It's as if He is showing me that when my mind gets renewed, there is space.

God doesn't tiptoe around the minefields in our heads, nor does He charge through them dictatorially. In His walk through my mind, He dignifies me and my story and this moment.

He knows the history of what I think and what I feel—years needing tending, secrets needing His touch, fears needing to be held in the night, not sermonized. He sees all forty-five years of my life in one glance and can hold both the little-girl me and the mom as He softly restores my mind. He heals while He holds me and my thoughts. His promise to "keep him in perfect peace, whose mind is stayed on [Him], because he trusts in [Him]" (Isa. 26:3 NKJV) does require something of us.

It's trust.

And growth in trust. How's that for nebulous? We want to trust God, we yearn for trust, but we reach for it like searching for a light switch in a dark room. We keep reaching, fumbling, pounding the wall. And yet I often wonder whether growing in trust is much simpler than we think: walk the path He has given us, like toddlers, unashamed of our need for reassurance and to be held. Charge ahead, tumble and scrape our knees and need a cuddle before taking the next step. We need much more of God's touch than our adult selves tell us.

And that touch is both His Spirit and His Word.

We need His Word for our minds to be newly angled toward trust.

————— *For Your Continued Pursuit* —————

Joshua 1:8 | Psalm 16:5–6 | Psalm 51:16–17 | Psalm 116:6–8 | Psalm 119:25 | Isaiah 26:3 | John 1:1–4 | John 16:13 | Romans 12:2 | 2 Corinthians 3:18 | 2 Corinthians 10:5 | Hebrews 4:12

Part 4

THE WONDER-FILLED BENEFITS OF STEPPING INTO GOD'S LIMITLESSNESS, LIMITED

THE WHIMSICAL NATURE OF RAINBOWS REMINDS ME that God adorns even the rain. This last group of chapters is for your whimsy—to dream again, but in a way that feels more tethered to His story than what you imagined your best story would be; to find the grass underneath your feet, within your fence line, and to wiggle your bare toes in it like a child who notices the feel of a ladybug crawling their skin or the feel of the crumbled earth in their palm; to smell the honeysuckle and climb the maple and discover, for the first time or again, the child within you who has been waiting to be fathered, to find home.

11

LIVING PRESENT

There is a day when the road neither comes nor goes,
and the way is not a way but a place.
—WENDELL BERRY, "THERE IS A DAY"

DISTILLING LIFE INTO A SINGLE MOMENT AND BEING ABLE
to taste, see, smell, and touch what that single moment holds is
a heart at rest within the boundaries. Our ability to be present
reveals how comfortable we feel sitting in His lap, in the yard
He gave us, despite the circumstances.

A birthday slid inside an especially tough year is bound to make
one more alert or dull—reaching for fireworks out of the hardness,
or numb to the possibility of anything good coming from the hardness. In this particular year, I was more alert. The months leading
up to my birthday were unexpectedly challenging, but as I assessed
my friends' landscapes, it was clear that unexpected challenges were
the new normal for so many of them.

This wasn't the first iteration of surprising hardness in my life.
God had a history of using the hardness to shape and form me, but

also to hold me. Because I learned to recognize this pattern over the years, new hardness was still hard but not debilitating. I had tools, and I had stories. Pages of my Bible bore wrinkles from my tears and had dated notes in the margin that I could look back on and see the exchange between God and me. The payoff was becoming more evident in my life—peace, presence of mind, growing steadiness— such that it was a tad bit easier to trust this next round of hardness wouldn't crush me, even though at times I felt crushed.

So on this birthday, I was alert. Notably needy, with a stance that asked, not desperately but hopefully, *God, show up for me today.* I knew He would.

The first sign came in the morning, early.

I padded barefoot out to my teapot in the dark, hours before— Lord willing—my family woke up. I poured Nate's coffee and picked up the birthday card propped against my teapot. Inside, Nate had written the word *release.* This word wasn't new to either of us. We'd talked for months about how God was preparing me, in my recent cycle of "come, die, grieve, live," to release something I'd held dear, something I didn't feel was meant to be released but knew He was asking me to relinquish. I likened it to Abraham, in my mind, desir- ing God alone and yet, of course, having to suffer the complexity of what God asked of him. It had to feel so wrong, so counter to his fatherly intuition, and yet he climbed Mount Moriah to sacrifice his son, Isaac. My legs felt heavy from a similar climb. It had been a year of climbing, releasing hopes and dreams that no mother wants to release.

Nate wrote a prayer for me, for my further release of my own "Isaac," for the strength of my climb, for my heavy legs and reluc- tant heart. I folded the card and went back to my morning routine, talking to God about the year ahead, considering release again for the umpteenth time.

Halfway through my birthday-morning quiet, I pulled the card out to reread it, wanting to absorb what the person who knows me best had to say about my year, and I noticed that on the front of the card was a garden.

This is a small thing, and I'm not one who savors the printed sentiments on store-bought cards, but I noticed this garden and thought, *How sweet. How happenstance.*

It was a three-dimensional card: the flowers were raised, as was the birdhouse that hung from the watercolor tree. The card was lush with color and butterflies. I know my husband well enough to know he didn't spend even three minutes selecting his card—he merely needed a clean place to write his words—and my attention to its details would have waned had I opened it about thirty minutes later when the little girls woke up, but at this moment I savored the sentiment I held in my hand.

I was alert. Present.

After thinking about the striking beauty of God's creation and a year that felt void of the beauty I'd desired, I noticed one more thing about the card. Around this garden was a white picket fence. The flowers grew up and around the fence, but they were encased by it.

I was sure Nate hadn't noticed this, and had he given me the card two hours later, I likely wouldn't have either, but in the quiet of my birthday morning, I realized the picture God was giving me. The release He'd asked of me this year—the painful surrender—had beauty, it was just fenced. And wasn't I coming to understand that this is the way with God's beauty?

It had boundary lines I didn't want and limits I wouldn't wish on anyone. I realized what I had felt this year of release was my bumping up against the fence line, the discomfort of God's no when I wanted a yes. I felt the disappointment of what I once would have called unanswered prayer but was growing to understand to be God's tender leadership.

The fence looked different this past year. Or maybe I was different. I noticed the flowers instead of the terrible discomfort of the hedge. I knew instinctively that this beauty had to be contained here. It was potent and vibrant, though smaller than I might have liked.

The morning turned holy.

I cried over the card, over God's reach for me. It felt like His accolade, as if to say, *Though contained, quelled, this beauty is a force.* And this time, I believed Him. His measure was best, His fence line needed.

This is the orchestra of trust. It grows one instrument at a time. We find relief in trust, in the sigh we finally give when we release, when we surrender. Then another place of mistrust, fear, and anxiety surfaces. We see it and our bodies finally feel what we've been ignoring. It feels terrible for a time until we slowly unfurl it from ourselves, and then we see what He creates—we trust. Then another instrument is added. First, strings. Then percussion, brass, filling out the symphony. It happens over decades—a lifetime—not over the days or months we are so accustomed to measuring.

We oversimplify trust as a one-and-done rather than a lifetime pursuit. But our generous God encourages us along the way. If we look for it, we will find it, and then we'll want to keep reaching for more. That fruit drives us to consider the next area He puts in front of us so that we might feel, see, talk to Him and engage His Word, grieve our losses and limitations, and eventually surrender.

We do this countless times. Trust grows slowly but steadily when we participate.

When asked why they processed the pain of their story and history, one of my children answered simply, "I just want peace."

This child voiced the angst that so many of us live under day after day after day, unnamed. We acquiesce to low-grade anxiety as if it has a permanent role in our narratives.

But His promise is perfect peace (Isa. 26:3). This peace comes from our trust.

Come (choose to step forward and not stay stuck), die (let Him have His way with us), grieve (collapse into God and don't forget our thwarted longings when we do), and live (truly live) unto greater trust. Again and again and again. And each time, one more instrument is added to the orchestra of our lives. We add layers and depth, the melody grows, and the overture comes together to produce a life song.

"At the cross," Philip Yancey writes, "hiddenness, ambiguity, and strange beauty converge."[1]

For six years, I led a small group of younger women that met in my family room twice a month. Sometimes it was once a month, and sometimes we took months-long breaks—it was that sort of group. We adjusted as one another's babies were born, and more babies were born, and I watched my first teenager graduate. We lived a lot of life in those six years. Several women grew their families from zero to three children. Those children grew, and I watched it all happen from my family-room sectional.

We vowed to end at nine thirty for the sake of the nursing moms and pregnant moms (not to mention this mom of teenagers who was going gray simply by existing in that season), but most

---

1. Philip Yancey, "Foreword," in Makoto Fujimura, *Silence and Beauty: Hidden Faith Born of Suffering* (Downers Grove, IL: InterVarsity Press, 2016), 18.

nights, I turned the last light off much later than that. We had so much to say, so much life to share, and everyone wanted a place and time when the struggles of motherhood and marriage and walking with God felt a little clearer. My couch fielded deep belly laughter and sobs during those years. None of us went without sharing a moment of loss among sisters.

Though I led the group, I'm confident I was the most blessed by it. These women set up spa and movie nights with my daughters when I was forty-two and pregnant and needed to go to bed at eight thirty, the time that most teenagers finally wake for the day. They played pranks on our family when we all needed a good laugh, and became experts at celebrating each other's vulnerable reaches for God. This group was neither perfect nor perfectly safe, but it was an attempt in a world where many of us long for a connection that doesn't just happen on accident.

And after five and a half years, I sensed the Lord asking me to lay it down. My typical decision-making paradigm didn't fit this request. These women were hungry for God and open with one another at a time when they desired mentorship. I loved them as if they were my younger sisters, sometimes overwhelmed by the care I felt in my heart for each one of them—crying over their losses, holding their pain with them, reaching for God for them.

It didn't make sense. We don't end good things, especially in a pressed world where good feels hard to find. God was moving, and we were growing. Isn't this the measurement that determines our continued yes?

Not always. God "assigned to the sea its limit, so that the waters might not transgress his command, when he marked out the foundations of the earth" (Prov. 8:29 ESV). He has "fixed all the boundaries of the earth; . . . [he] made summer and winter"

(Ps. 74:17 ESV). He chooses the land's end and where the rivulets form. He creates islands and inlets and peninsulas.

And sometimes, He ends the very best of things.

We gathered around my table for a feast on the night of our last meeting. A tablescape of eucalyptus and twinkling tea lights set the stage for our winter soups, which we ate out of homemade bread bowls, each of us wanting to set this night apart and I wanting to remember it as if in a snow globe, dazzling, preserved, always available to hold.

I cried with them, fumbling to express the depth of emotion I felt for these women and my confusion that in our "sage" years, Nate and I continued to hear nos from God regarding our commitments and investments outside our home. Our leadership in this season felt most natural, the least striving, that we'd known it to be, yet the whisper of the Lord continued to be *not yet, not now.* Even this beautifully fruitful group of women, a group that thrived for years, became a *no longer.*

The mystery of God becomes less of a hindrance and more of a wonder as we surrender to the stories He has written for our lives. I grieved the loss of this group and the regular gathering in my family room and all that I loved about hosting women who wanted a brief reprieve from the chaos of motherhood. I grieved all the parts of it—their hearts, shared with me and each other, the uniqueness of their hunger for God, the hospitality. Even the seasons of snacks— chocolate mousse, whipped cream, and fruit in the summer after a long winter of hot chai.

But in the loss, there was a mystery, a mystery that felt wonderfully freeing—wonder and not angst, openhandedness and not clinging, clutching. I wonder whether part of this group's ending was so that I could experience a fence line that produced curiosity and not anger. *Is this maturity in God? Is this what happens when we lean into His chest with our lives—our forever Daddy?*

Home was becoming the yard He gave me, the acreage around which He put the boundary, the place He told me to put my feet. *My* green grass, dandelions and all, not my neighbors'. Home was becoming Him, and the peace of this kind of trust was intoxicating at times. Like my child, I too had craved this peace.

Henri Nouwen writes, "Faith is the radical trust that home has always been there and always will be there."[2]

I was finding home, and I was growing in that radical trust. It didn't require enormous willpower, because I simply needed to let Him wrap His fingers around mine and lead me toward surrender. I needed merely to submit to the cycle of "come, die, grieve, live" again.

Surrendering, I approached a single minute as a child would: attentive, present, wide eyed, expectant.

It's four thirty in the afternoon—the roof-raising hour in our home. Bo, Virginia, and Charlotte have set up lanes for Bo's Matchbox cars that stretch from the second-floor banister down to the first-story fireplace. Most cars won't make it to the finish, but the children assure me they've positioned pillows in all of the places the cars might stray so as not to leave dents on the walls and baseboards.

Caleb is tinkering on the piano—something from Billy Joel he's been playing by ear for years, and always when he's bored—and I'm wondering whether Lily, working on a painting one story below, can hear him and whether it's disruptive to her creative process. Hope

---

2. Henri Nouwen, *The Return of the Prodigal Son: A Story of Homecoming* (New York: Doubleday, 1994), 39.

and Eden are talking in the kitchen, laughing loudly and interrupting each other and oblivious to my cooking, inching toward where I'm chopping onions and then between me and the sink.

It's not just their oblivious bodies that I'm navigating around. I keep tripping over the dog—the dog I bought for Nate as a surprise for his birthday who keeps desperately and unsuccessfully trying to win my affection by following at my heels wherever I go.

It's the kind of afternoon that threatens to irk me—noises, lots of them and disparate, interrupting my once-quiet kitchen. Twenty minutes earlier, I was chopping ingredients with care and getting lost in that sweet intermingling of prayer and thought. Now I am revisiting the recipe I keep misplacing as I'm distracted by Hope and Eden's conversation and the sound of the cars racing from the second floor, hoping they don't break my new Pottery Barn lamp, which had been on backorder for four months before it finally arrived.

But I'm not irked today. I'm absorbing this moment. I love when Caleb tinkers with the keys; it's my favorite expression of boredom. Eden and Hope have a rare intertwining of friendship circles, and their goofy antics make me laugh, too. Virginia is Bo's accomplice, and Bo feels strong and leaderlike, protecting Char from the flying cars. And when Lily paints, our home feels like what it's supposed to be—a canvas holding beauty, emerging alongside accidental paint splotches on upholstered chairs.

If I'd been interrupted by sending three texts at once, multitasking, and the anxiety that crept in that morning, I would have missed the way the sun came through our second-story window as it began to set and hit Char's curls, making them look golden, aflame. I would have missed that my fifteen-year-old still tinkers on the keys, even though he will dress for a football game on Saturday. I would have missed that this very unkempt moment, which was keeping me from the quiet life I think I need most, is holy.

We want to make the everyday minutes holy—something in us tells us that these middle minutes matter—but it takes something like a thousand steps to get there.

We dance around concepts like being present and celebrating the small and turning up the microscope on the minuscule movements of our day. These are important, but they're the fruit. We can practice them, but we won't fully embrace their purpose if we don't first walk the road it takes to receive them.

Being present—able to notice little-girl feet as they stand on tippy-toes and the way Nate's shoulders shake when I say something that makes him laugh hard; able to revel in Bo's running football plays with himself, barefoot in crisp Decembered grass—is the wonderful byproduct of surrendering to the limited life God gives me. The air is translucent here, and even the noisiest days feel notable, not debilitating.

We can practice being present to what is right in front of us, but the fullest form of being present comes almost accidentally as we learn to lean. Trust teaches us how to be present. Not overnight, not willed, but over time and with steady attention to our hearts and His heart as we face our limits, as we create space in our minds to see a single minute and all that it carries.

My ability to be present to a certain moment is a helpful gauge for my heart. I realize that I spent many, many years of my life distracted. I listened to a hurting friend as if on an airport runway, unable to fully hear because of all the noise. As David Benner writes, I know that "I cannot really be present for another person when my inner world is filled with preoccupations and distractions."[3]

"But I have calmed and quieted my soul, like a weaned child

---

3. David G. Benner, *Sacred Companions: The Gift of Spiritual Friendship and Direction* (Downers Grove, IL: InterVarsity Press, 2002), 47.

with its mother; like a weaned child is my soul within me" (Ps. 131:2 ESV).

That child is held and known. There will be a response to every one of her needs; she knows this. With a mere cry, she invokes rocking and holding and kissing and feeding. Of course her soul is calm. She is known, watched, and guarded by the mother who made her.

To return to that childlike place is the resounding cry of our souls.

It requires a life's work, but not one that is impossible.

The habit of clearing the cache, of bringing our thoughts into alignment with His Word and decluttering our minds, gains strength over hours, days, weeks, and years until it becomes like brushing our teeth, almost unthinkingly done. As the fruit of being present grows, even within firm fence lines and surprisingly disappointing limits, we have more motivation to give more and more of our six thousand thoughts to God and lean with our lives.

Being present enables me to absorb times such as this: One afternoon I found myself having a different dialogue with God over the same occurrences that once annoyed me. The rhythm of afternoon quiet in our home while babies nap and bigger kids read typically meant time for my heart to decompress, even for three minutes. I worked this muscle of unwinding, bringing the little splinters of my day under His attentive eye. But on this day, instead of a repetitive ache—lack of time, energy, ability to meet all my children's needs, and peace and quiet—I looked over my shoulder at the week before and, unthinking, noticed surprise deliveries from God.

- The teenagers all happened to be out one evening after the little ones were in bed, and Nate and I found ourselves with hours, not minutes, to chat and then even extra time to read novels.

- Somehow in my very full day, I found time to finally organize the stack of printed recipes that had been sitting on my desk for two years; I'd intended that "next week" I'd put them somewhere. I filed, systemized, and put them all in a binder. (Creating order and systems is a secret love that often goes untended with my house chaos.)

- I ordered new novels from the library and finished the page-turner whose pages I hadn't been turning. *Where did the time come from?*

- Last minute, I threw together ingredients for a pie that *everyone* loved.

If my cache is cluttered, I miss these everyday moments. They happen and I'm mindlessly not noticing. When my mind is clear, I am present to them. Receiving.

Looking back over my shoulder at the week, I was overwhelmed with gratitude. Yes, it's a practice that is good and needed and promising, but when the well is deep and hits the water just right, attention to detail and gratitude for that detail *becomes* the overflow.

The more I walk through the "come, die, grieve, live" cycle, again and again, the more I trust the one who is leading, not merely participating in, my life, and the more grateful I am to be known.

And present.

I embrace the role of a passenger, alert and present to her surroundings, but not to worries with the road. It feels right and holy and whole.

——— *For Your Continued Pursuit* ———

Genesis 22:1–19 | Psalm 36:7–9 | Psalm 74:17 | Psalm 131:2 |
Proverbs 8:29 | Isaiah 26:3 | Matthew 6:25–34 | Matthew 18:3–4 |
2 Corinthians 4:8–12 | 2 Corinthians 10:5

A Better Way

Becoming Ourselves

> Glorious indeed is the world of God around us, but
> more glorious the world of God within us.
> —Henry Wadsworth Longfellow, *Hyperion*

Some people daydream about what they haven't
had.

On the other hand, I catch myself replaying an earlier time in
my life as if I could will it back and live my present life in the background of this earlier reality.

This daydream comes from nearly twenty years ago. Nate and
I had crawled across our finish line of full-time ministry, one that
came much too early. We retired out of tiredness, the ultimate walk
of shame for those who had planned to stay a lifetime in full-time
ministry. We were not only tired but unsure of who we were when
we didn't have a job description that included "advancing the kingdom of God." Nate started what he called a "jobby-job," and I scaled

back to part-time work for a paycheck. I worked in a little boutique on North Barracks Road in Charlottesville, Virginia, selling French and Italian pottery for minimum wage to clients who made much more than minimum wage.

At first, we both felt demoted—leaving the hall of fame of ministry we'd created in our minds. But then my heart started coming alive in the extra hours, the longer transition times between activities, and the evenings at home with regular bedtimes.

I rediscovered the little girl in me who loves stories. Just like when I was twelve, I began devouring books. We prayed together at night and sometimes even brought out the guitar and sang worship songs. I poked around stores on my days off and lingered longer over coffee with friends. I journaled and cooked recipes out of the Martha Stewart cookbook that had served, before that time, only as a decoration to my kitchen.

Life was slow and savory.

We slept late on the weekends, kept a sabbath that didn't include changing diapers or refereeing sibling squabbles, and took hours-long walks together through the rambling streets of the old Virginia college town where we lived.

I can remember the fall of that year as if it were yesterday. I have more memories of that one fall than I do of the four before them combined. Soups on the stove, lit candles around our little cottage as we read at night, friends over for long dinners—my heart slowly revived to sounds and smells and images of beauty that God had given me but that I'd been too driven to notice.

It was a rebuilding and rediscovery time. We both knew it. We lived and thrived in a state of rest, slowly inching our way out into the world (a new church plant, new ministries with our neighbors), carrying cups that sloshed over with fullness.

Those were dreamy times. Ones that filled me then and fill my mind now.

But life has changed. We understood a different kind of fence line when we added two young children to our family, and then two more not long after. Somehow, ten years passed and we filled this house with more people than can legally ride in a minivan—seven lives to grow, plus us and a canine. Though our home dramatically changed, my picture of rest did not.

In time, I realized that I'd been applying the same grid for rest to my seven-child life, and I'd been doing it for more than a decade. We do that, don't we? We taste a moment of being fully alive and fully ourselves, and we're sure that the landscape is what made us that way. So we keep reaching back. Just like Peter said to Jesus when he saw the blazing light of the sun on His face, "Lord, it is good that we are here. If you wish, I will make three tents here, one for you and one for Moses and one for Elijah" (Matt. 17:4 ESV), we want to stay where we experience God at His brightest and He bathes us in that light.

Many of us are reaching for that rest of the soul where we feel at home in what God made and at peace with the moment like it's a rounded stone heading downhill, faster still each day. We can't nab it or catch up to it, but it's still in sight, so we'd better race after it. Or maybe we catch it and hold it for a moment before it slides right back out of our hands in our ever-downhill life. We grow more tired pursuing that time when we once felt ourselves.

In my efforts toward that soul rest, I have worked myself out of rest.

The real rest.

The better rest.

We all do that in one way or another. We fixate on a time in our lives that was glorious and restful and we felt alive and unchallenged in our bodies and minds and schedules. Or if we haven't yet experienced a time like that, we fantasize about what it must be like, ever reaching for the dream of a forever sabbatical. We see friends who have found rest within this crazy cultural moment, and we envy them. We envy a person at rest and at peace within themselves—a person who is confident and present—but we overlook the fact that that person's ability to be present and alive and even joyful in the moment is often *not* because of their circumstances. They've cultivated a better rest of the soul.

Nate and I traveled recently, and every airport was jammed with people as if it were spring break—women in athleisure wear and men in Hawaiian shirts carrying bags from the T-shirt shops where they acquired their travel trinkets. Business travel hadn't picked up even years after the COVID quarantines, but the thirst for vacation was indicative of the world's reach to do something—anything—to quell the daily chaos.

It sometimes takes years of movement in one direction, with no shifting, before I see my stuckness as something God-ordained. Finally, out of this years-long chase for rest, a phrase dropped into my mind that led me to consider whether my legs really need to be faster and my intellect more informed, whether I really need to live an earlier season again.

The better rest.

With one phrase, the air clears a bit.

God offers something that's available even to the mom of seven (who can't take a kid off her "full plate"), the daughter tirelessly caring for her sick father, the husband of a wheelchair-bound wife, the father working the night shift to pay rent, the new mom of twins, the single woman in her fifties with a lot of time and also a lot of anxiety that she can't put on hold during her sabbath.

The better rest comes to one who knows themselves within the context of God's story for them, the rest of the dreamer who is leaning into God's vision with Him. Not a romantic rest, dependent on the external, but something welling up from within.

The rest of a settled soul.

There is a story of a Hasidic rabbi who cried on his deathbed, "When I get to heaven, I will not worry so much if God asks me, 'Zusya, why were you not more like Abraham?' or 'Zusya, why where you not more like Moses?' I know I would be able to answer those questions. . . . But what will I say when God asks me, 'Zusya, why were you not more like Zusya?'"[1]

Untold amounts of energy spent studying the fence lines of our lives and how to circumvent them steals the real pursuit: exploring Him and His story written and unfolding inside of us.

You have lines on your fingertips that have no match. The way your eyes are placed on your face and offset your nose and, at times, highlight the wrinkles in your forehead just above them or the dimple on your right cheek below them is like no one else's eyes. You may be one of millions of middle children or eldest born, but no one on the earth carries the same thoughts that you do.

The "come, die, grieve, live" cycle gently inches us toward not merely seeing our uniqueness but finding our settled place within God's story, the part of the narrative written for only one person. The more we surrender and settle into Him, the less we strive to make it happen and, instead, receive and co-dream with Him

---

1. Sylvia Rothschild, "Twenty-Third Elul: The Question We Will Be Asked in Heaven: Why Were You Not You?" rabbisylviarothschild.com, September 23, 2019, https://rabbi sylviarothschild.com/tag/why-were-you-not-zusya.

because we are known, because we are seen, because we are loved as we are.

Surrender moves this knowledge from a page or a Bible study or a sermon to somewhere deep within our souls. It opens our ears to the continual whisper, *You are loved and valued just as you are.*

Knowing and accepting ourselves is a lifelong pursuit, but one that has legs: it moves us forward. More than pages on a calendar are these minuscule movements of the heart where we understand a bit more today than we did yesterday that we are deeply cherished by the one whose hands formed our fingerprints.

It's here that the settled rest comes in ever-increasing measure, and with it comes the real stuff of dreams: the narrative of God, expanding inside of us, expanding us.

I learned over years that I carry my anxiety with me to the beach. For some reason, I can't leave it behind, and I bring unnamed expectations into my vacations. I think I'll come home more rested and alive with memories to cover over dozens of future pull-my-hair-out moments.

Our family trip to Maui was no different. We knew this was likely a once-in-a-lifetime event. Some people go to the islands as a habit; we go as a luxury.

As I spent a week packing for nine of us to cross the ocean, my memory returned to childhood dreaming, reaching for a time when all would be settled and the most significant challenge would be keeping sand outside of the beach house and our suitcases. Even as early as eight, I remember feeling like the beach would solve all my problems. I met God there in my teenage years and continued to build a narrative around a landscape-driven rest from all cares.

So I imagined Maui to be a struggle-free zone. Sure, we'd be jet lagged and have our sleep disturbed by changing time zones, but I forgot for a flash that the aches of childhood trauma are not long stifled by surfing lessons and ice-cream cones. They even come to the beach.

Two days into our trip, I found my heart distracted. It was the night we drove for nearly an hour to take a boat out on the ocean to watch for whales. Though the excursion was a tourist attraction, the beauty wasn't muted for any of us. These majestic creatures flipped, breached, and spouted just feet from our boat as the sun started to set in the distance. My littlest children, still enamored by squirrels in our yard, who shout when they see a cardinal or a chickadee at the feeder, stood stunned, eyes fixed on the water. We saw mamas and babies and pods dancing as if for our approval.

This night should have felt distilled in time as I watched the unrestrained wonder of my youngest ones and the newly awakened wonder of my sometimes sleepy teenagers, but I was distracted. We were in Maui, but we didn't leave struggle behind. Here it was, inside my chest and taking up space in my head, clouding wonder.

I was both reactive and distracted, not thoughtful about it. But then, three, four, and five days into our trip, I realized I might lose myself in Maui, just like I can lose myself at home with the Monday-morning anxiety that comes as I stare ahead at the week of endless needs and responsibilities. *Well, shoot, real life slipped into my suitcase on this trip, now, didn't it?*

With the help of Nate's steady voice in my ear and my extra-long quiet hours of the morning, which came early because my body refused to adjust to island time, God drew my attention to my distracted heart. I moved from staying stuck under my circumstances—praying that this hiccup in our trip would just shift—to talking to God about them. The more I lamented this ache, the more present I grew: taking hours-long walks with Nate along the coastline, reflecting on the year, talking about the year ahead; scanning the horizon for more whales; being still with my little ones as they played in the ocean; savoring acai bowls and paddleboarding and all that came with our ocean days. The more I named this circumstantial ache that wasn't lifting, the less power it had to distract me. It was still there, pulling on my heart, but not in the undefined times.

Finally, on one of the last afternoons of our trip, I slid away for a few hours. I found a secluded spot with a manicured lawn and a bench at the water's edge. Everywhere I looked, I saw a beauty that touched more than my eyes. I smelled the ocean and felt it on my skin. I saw whale spouts in the far distance, and rounds of deep blue striking the rocks and turning into cascades of white just below me. Mountains, in shadow with the bright sun behind them, served as a backdrop.

My first response was, "But *this*, God. This hard thing. You brought us all the way to Maui and . . . and . . . *this*. Why can't the beach of my childhood dreams, where all gets washed away with the tide, be my reality? How could we come all the way here, after days of packing and traveling and thousands of dollars spent, to have *this*?"

My place of peace, our scheduled vacation from trouble, held some of the hardest moments. Wasn't there a place on the other side of the fence away from all of this strife?

I said again, in my journal and my head, "You brought us all the way to Maui and . . . and . . . *this*!" A question and a statement: "How could You, God?"

And just then, in my mind, the emphasis shifted. The phrase was the same, my lament was the same, but His response was in the emphasis: "This happened, *and* I brought you to Maui." And again, "*This* happened [He heard my ache], *and* I brought you to Maui." A whisper, as if it was too sacred to be heard aloud: *and*.

There will always be *this*—some form of struggle or strife that distracts and attempts to steal sleep, peace, promise, and hope. It will travel with you to North Carolina beaches and pop up on your wedding day and your first day of grad school and remind you of its presence as you sleep with the windows open in late May. It will even come to Maui.

But this chain around your ankle attempting to make you clunky and slow and distracted, disrupting Maui—that's not the real story.

The real story: *And* you have a God who takes you to Maui despite *this thing*.

Ocean views and whales breaching are beautiful, but not as substantive as the whispers deep in your heart creating songs in places you never knew could sing. This is the work of our God. It can come in a suburban-sprawl back yard or on a sweltering August day in New York City when even the trash sweats. My Maui and yours is the back yard He gives us inside the fence line. The narrative merely needs His emphasis.

"You have this hard thing, Sara, *and* I brought you to Maui."

I worshiped that day overlooking the rocks. And it was perhaps one of the more worshipful moments I'd had in years. In the persistent ache that blistered on our trip, I hadn't overlooked Bible reading and whispered minute prayers and churchgoing, but I think I lost my song somewhere in there, my worship to God. And I suppose it didn't feel like much of a loss until I found it again—that deep, guttural "I need nothing more than I need You" worship—and remembered that I am most alive when I worship.

Finally alive.

"According to His abundant and boundless mercy, [He] has caused us to be born again." That's how 1 Peter 1:3 reads in the Amplified Bible. Peter goes on to say, "[That is, to be reborn from above— spiritually transformed, renewed, and set apart for His purpose] to an ever-living hope and confident assurance." I can canonize this and make it feel separate and distant from where I am, but it's personal.

Eugene Peterson in *The Message* says it this way: "Because Jesus was raised from the dead, we've been given a brand-new life and have everything to live for, including a future in heaven—and the future starts now! God is keeping careful watch over us and the future."

His careful watch makes me new at forty-five just like it did at fifteen. Not a one-and-done but an ever-renewing, constantly-doing-and-undoing aliveness in me. As Eugene Peterson writes, "God is continuously in action in ways that are comprehensively glorious."[2]

Everything is subject to this Man, this God-man. Everything. From my life to yours and all in between them. God architects the fence. He orchestrates the details. The more this settles inside of me, the more I settle. But it cannot be merely imparted to my mind. It must be sown into my life. He lays the blueprint for the fence in the context of my story. I listen on a Sunday morning to a sermon that reaffirms what I heard earlier in the week on a podcast and read just a few days later in a book, but none of this impacts me like when my sprinting body bumps up against this fence and I get interrupted by God. All of life is a series of these interruptions, my plans averted by

---

2. Eugene Peterson, *Practice Resurrection: A Conversation on Growing Up in Christ* (Grand Rapids: Eerdmans, 2013), 109.

His. My timeline delayed, my fears taking flight, the people in my world "misbehaving" according to what I want or need from them— all unto this ever-unfolding brand-new life.

And just like a brilliant architect, God is keeping careful watch so that I might rest as it happens—as it happens *to* me, often against my wishes. My floundering just might be part of His design.

This is citizenship. I slowly relinquish the heritage of my flesh, I flounder, and as I do I receive a new kind of citizenship—gradually being renewed, slowly gaining confidence, slowly feeling and living set apart, slowly gaining hope, slowly taking on a new home as my forever home.

And more deeply at rest, to boot.

God gave Adam boundaries—not punitively but as a Father who created life. "You may surely eat of every tree of the garden, but of the tree of the knowledge of good and evil you shall not eat, for in the day that you eat of it you shall surely die" (Gen. 2:16–17 ESV).

And thousands of generations later, I—Adam's daughter—walk a lifetime learning, more and more still, that God's parameters help me find the best life in the garden He made for me.

This is home-finding, home-settling, and home-establishing. I flounder. God leads.

This is becoming God's daughter, His pigtailed, safe, and secure little girl.

It's rest in its actual form.

Feeling loved, seen, and known can make us surprisingly vulnerable. Beginning to wear our citizenship—to be settled as one who was made and is not making themselves, as one who is boundaried by God and, though reluctantly at times, welcomes being a child—in many ways makes us more comfortable with being human. The older I get, the less I blush at my mistakes or try to right a wrong quickly. I say "of course" about my failings more than "how could I?!" I am less surprised by myself and live vulnerable to the elements more often than not.

My most recent birthday was the best that I can remember since my sweet sixteen, when two of my best friends and I filled a pool with our closest friends and sang songs into the fleeting summer air at dark with fall just around the corner.

It was as if a layer of skin had been peeled back and I could feel everything. I woke to intentionality from Nate—that card with the fenced garden, his prayer for me written inside—and my favorite breakfast food. I savored all of it, feeling how he sees me and reveling in being seen. Throughout the day came thoughtful, prayerful texts, meaningful gifts, and sweet, surprise generosity from my kids and friends. I felt full—after so many birthdays when I peered over the fence.

This year I changed diapers and refereed squabbles and felt seen, known, and settled. I sat with Nate on the back porch as the sun set and felt at home in my skin, with him, in this crazy life.

It's strange to have our desires met, and because they so often aren't for various reasons, we live bracing ourselves for the worst, as if we don't want them met because that would give permission to joy, hope, and expectancy, and those three things are scary.

I wanted this day and this night of settledness for so long, yet I also fought it for that same length of time, unknowingly sabotaging the thing I craved most. This is an orphan way: we fear joy, because tasting it while knowing it might be fleeing is just as scary as, if not scarier than, living without it. Becoming ourselves is scary, because the peace and joy that come with God's settling us can feel so unfamiliar. What if we taste them and they leave?

There have been times in my life when things finally started to feel serene, and instead of blessing the moment and enjoying that gift, I found myself stirring up dust—giving in to worry or meddling or anxious forecasting. These responses too often go unexamined, but on this birthday, I saw how I accidentally—though maybe intentionally—can pattern my life against the trajectory of God: peace.

Jesus said, "Peace I leave with you; my peace I give to you. Not as the world gives do I give to you. Let not your hearts be troubled, neither let them be afraid" (John 14:27 ESV).

Sometimes we create our own limits as we mitigate our vulnerability when we recognize God's limitlessness. We are exposed, and He comes near. We are so accustomed to shunning boundaries that being thrust into the safety of being a daughter or son invigorates parts of our souls into unfamiliarity.

God's dream of us is not new. His dream of our floundering, fumbling, but reaching a life lived within His boundaries is not new. He dreams of our living well within our boundaries. But our receiving it *is* new. These are the days of new-to-us dreams, the ones He held all along, but that we are receiving for the first time.

And for once in our lives, as David Benner writes, "the goal is God, not growth."[3]

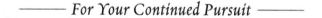

——— *For Your Continued Pursuit* ———

Genesis 2:16–17 | Isaiah 64:8 | Matthew 6:26 | Matthew 17:4 | John 14:27 | Philippians 3:20–21 | 1 Peter 1:3

---

3. David G. Benner, *Opening to God:* Lectio Divina *and Life as Prayer* (Downers Grove, IL: InterVarsity Press, 2021), 144.

—— 13 ——

SOMETHING BEYOND

You have loved us first, O God, alas! . . . When we wake up in the morning and turn our soul toward You—You are there first—You have loved us first; if I rise at dawn and at the same second turn my soul toward You in prayer, You are there ahead of me. You have loved me first.

—SØREN KIERKEGAARD, *THE PRAYERS OF KIERKEGAARD*

THE FIRST YEAR AFTER I BEGAN A PERSONAL RELATION-ship with God, I noticed things around our home that had always been there but now had new meanings. For the first time, I found the crucifix my mom hung on the wall in our foyer when we moved in years before; I passed it every day on my way out the door, but this time I noticed it. I opened the family Bible in our living room and heard the spine crack. My mom received a weekly magazine, just larger than my palm, with devotionals from the Bible and other religious things like advertisements for rosaries and tours to the Holy Land. One particular week, I noticed that the cover included a ruddy-faced

Jesus. His lips were red and vibrant. His eyes glistened and seemed to move with me as I held the magazine at different angles. He looked fresh off the tennis courts, his skin tanned and his feathered hair slightly sweaty.

I was bold to speak up in Bible study that week, even though I was new to attend: "And I just love that God made Jesus attractive." A junior girl, a year older than me and a decade wiser—she quoted Scripture in school and read her Bible between classes—was quick to counter, "No, Jesus actually wasn't physically attractive."

What? I thought, remembering the image and still too new to following God to know there were other sources of information than the weekly *Liguorian* magazine—namely the Bible. She quoted Isaiah 53:2 to me: "He had no form or majesty that we should look at him, and no beauty that we should desire him" (ESV).

Huh. Well, I really liked the idea of God being attractive.

Beautiful, even.

The decades ahead revealed, though, that despite His not being a head turner, God was beautiful.

"Christianity," writes C. S. Lewis, "seems at the first to be all about morality, all about duties, and the rules and guilt and virtue, yet it leads you on, out of all that, into something beyond. One has a glimpse of a country where they do not talk of those things. . . . But this is near the stage where the road passes over the rim of our world."[1]

The rim of our world lacks depth. We don't see this until we

---

1. C. S. Lewis, *Mere Christianity*, C. S. Lewis Signature Classics (New York: HarperCollins, 2017), 123.

skin our knees against it and realize there might be another road and, perhaps, it passes beyond what we conceive of as the "exceedingly, abundantly, above all that we ask or think" of Ephesians.

We imagine God's idea of abundance to be an exaggerated version of ours, like an upgraded hotel room or a surprise free drink at our favorite coffee shop. And while He sometimes does those very things, His way often confounds.

One December, in a stretch of days that didn't feel twinkly and full of Christmas promise, God reminded me of *His* ways. We had rain for days, with no sun. The clouds weren't snow filled, just gray. Outside my front door mirrored my insides. It was a long December that year, cradling the stories of children whose hearts broke before they were big enough to break their arms climbing trees. As the years had turned into more than a decade of seeing the impacts of generational trauma, my heart felt sobered and grieved. Again. Just as I ached that their early childhoods felt significantly different from their friends', whose first steps were counted and first words recorded, I ached that I continued to fumble through this unconventional motherhood without a script.

As another morning revealed a sunless sunrise, I remembered this: life in God is not a one-and-done. The inertia of my thinking and the world I live in lead me to live as if all victories are once won and all growth is behind us. But God ordained the earth to rotate and to produce the cycle of seasons, just as He did our lives.

Returning to Middle America in my adulthood reminded me that every November is a mix of surprising warmth and surprising cold, and that every March, I want to put on flip-flops and expose my toes to the air at the sight of the first early bloom. "As long as the earth endures, seedtime and harvest, cold and heat, summer and winter, day and night will never cease" (Gen. 8:22). Life is cyclical.

Jesus promised us trouble in the world (John 16:33), but He

also promised that He would overcome the world. Nobody would have thought that the way to overcome was through death. And here I was on this gray Tuesday morning in December, remembering again that just as God cycles the earth through seasons, He cycles my life through loss, grief, and resurrection over and over. It is His way.

You and I will face boundaries and limitations—painful, arduous ones that elicit resentment—every season and often by surprise. It may take substantial pain before we see that life ends with death and that Saturday's grief, if experienced, will produce the best Sunday we've ever known, over and over again. We will live the same narrative dozens of hundreds of times in our lifetimes, but against a different backdrop every time.

But the end of it all—and every single time—involves a Man much more beautiful than the sun-kissed tennis player in my mother's magazine.

It was Nate's sabbatical week. February gave us sixty-five degrees and sunny for the first half of his week at home with us, perfect for family walks and basketball on the driveway and pushing our littlest people on the swing. I look forward to this week, when we have extra-long "dates" in the morning, our time together bleeding like watercolors outside the schedule, and take slow sips of life. Except this particular week, I was sick. And then Nate was ill. And then, like dominoes, each of our children went down with the same sickness. I didn't step outside for two days. I watched spring's dress rehearsal through my bedroom window.

Half the week passed, and we all shuffled through our days in pajamas and bedheads. The sickness finally lifted, followed by a downpour lasting for days. *Figures.* It was the first morning of Lent, a new season, the one when we walk the road of the cross in our hearts. And here I was again, walking it in my life.

I opened my psalter, a gift from a friend, to read this: "What does it mean that believers will see the face of God? It means we will become ourselves, finally. It means dawn will rise on the dark gray of this fallen world. It means final rest will be ours. . . . As the very end of the Bible puts it: 'They will see his face' (Revelation 22:4)."[2]

If this whole life builds to the moment when we get to see His face, why do we spend a lifetime reaching for something else and expect to—*boom*—acquire a taste for the beauty of His face the moment we make that step into eternity? Most of us live this way.

That gray morning, reading about the coming dawn and knowing my desire for a fresh dawn that day, I knew what my heart needed. This Man. This God who took on flesh and walked among us. I needed to see the look on His face as I walked the way of the cross with my children, to see how He watched me when I fumbled through another valley. I needed to see the weight in His eyes as He beheld His daughter and as He held me.

Sometimes at night, I go into the room of our youngest two and watch them sleep. Their bodies are still in the night—no fussing or fighting or spilling-over enthusiasm. Watching them in their stillness, I remember Virginia's poetic language and Charlotte's strength in spirit and body. I can barely contain my affection as I look at them, holding what feels like a whole lifetime for them in my heart. I see my baby girls as they are now and as they will grow to be one day. I ache to pick them up, snuggle their bodies close against my skin, and run my fingers through their hair, still wet

---

2. Dane Ortlund, *In the Lord I Take Refuge: 150 Daily Devotions through the Psalms* (Wheaton, IL: Crossway, 2021), 36.

from the bath. I want to smell their sleep sweat and kiss the baby fat around Char's wrist.

I wonder about God's face when I sleep. His look down the corridor of my day, with a view beyond the rim of my life. I wonder what He notices that I don't, how I might chide myself for what I didn't do in a moment, but He sees that moment differently. I wonder if He loves the scent of my still shower-wet hair or wants to trace my fingernails or my freckles like I do my girls', unthinkingly, when I hold their hands or their faces in my hands.

God loved His children with this consuming love far before I felt it for my children. And while Revelation talks about seeing His face one day, we can see glimpses of it now. I'm invited, like the psalmist, to see His face—the God who spoke to Moses "face to face, as a man speaks to his friend" (Ex. 33:11 ESV). "Your face, LORD, do I seek" (Ps. 27:8 ESV) is a prayer for today.

It's like a hike that Nate and I used to do every year for our anniversary.

"Old Rag" in Virginia has an elevation of about 2,500 feet, which is relatively high for the Blue Ridge Mountains. Nine miles long, the hike takes a good portion of the day, but because those were our younger years and we lived only about an hour from the base of the mountain, we hiked to the top each year, timing ourselves. We had a set of traditions that we adhered to on this anniversary hike, but what I remember most is the view at the top. Two or three times during the trek we'd catch a glimpse of what we'd see at the top, but for much of our plodding our view was just rows of forestry. We hiked it not because it was rigorous but for that view and those glimpses en route.

It's a picture of my life in God: climbing, plodding, often without a view but knowing that a view is coming, that vistas along the way will spur us on. The view at the end is our goal, and the promise of His face gives us endurance, but I suppose I'm an anxious girl on Christmas morning who appreciates a stocking before the presents.

The flashes of His face, watching me watching Him, enable endurance. They are the best of life within the fence line. Eve hid in the garden from the one who knew where she was yet still asked, "Where are you?" God searches to find because He put in us a craving to be found. And that place where we're found, where we see Him seeing us, is inside His fence line.

Two thirty on one Tuesday afternoon produced no such flashes in my home.

Short ribs were cooking in the crockpot as Charlotte slept upstairs, the hum of her noisemaker bringing the ocean to Middle America. Bo was reading in his bedroom. About every thirty minutes or so, I'd hear a loud thump. I imagined him jumping off his dresser or whirling in the hammock that hung from his ceiling and hitting the wall; even boys with their noses in books for hours need to move their bodies. Virginia made treasures out of the scraps of paper left over from my wrapping presents, and my big kids were all out of the house. Our dog, Darcy, snored, lying in the one ray of sunlight coming through the second-story window in our vaulted family room. And I sat down to talk to God.

I'd made a habit of this midday and midevening "interruption"—what many call the daily office. Just a few minutes to divert my attention from the need in front of me and up to Him seemed to calibrate my life more than I'd thought it would when I started this habit.

I started with two minutes of silence, which quickly turned into lament. It was easy to lament these days as my big kids' hearts hurt, and I had many misgivings about how we fumbled to cradle them. I hurt for them—what they'd lost in their earliest years, the often-unnamed longing inside of them to belong to ones who shared their genes, the way some things in life were harder for them than their friends because of a history they didn't choose. I was lamenting these losses for them when it felt like the wall I was staring at as I prayed became a looking glass.

In a few seconds, I felt the warmth of understanding and knowing surrounding me. It came from outside of myself. I opened my Bible to read the lineup of my daily psalms, and here is what I read: "O Lord, you hear the desire of the afflicted; you will strengthen their heart; you will incline your ear to do justice to the fatherless and the oppressed" (Ps. 10:17–18 ESV).

He sees them. He sees their affliction. He hears their cries, and mine for them. His promise is justice and strengthening.

But the warmth of understanding and knowing, this looking glass of a moment, was that I knew it was *me* He saw at this moment. He saw my mama-ache, all the ways I couldn't reach them because of their pain. He saw the cracks in my motherhood, the ways I felt ill-equipped to reach them in their pain. He saw where I failed and where I kept trying not to fail and the exhaustion that emerged from attempting the impossible over and over again, from wishing with my whole being that I wouldn't be so limited in reaching them, so impotent to love them the way it seems they need to be loved. He received me in the helplessness, the powerlessness I felt in the face of a life and a dream and a hope well beyond the rim of my world.

My experience in His Word and with His presence in that moment—the warmth of a Father wrapping His strong arms around my shoulders and pulling me into His chest—changed the landscape. *I'd stay here if I could have more of this,* I thought. I am incompetent at times to parent such trauma, inept at reaching through the gated parts of my children's hearts, unable to heal with my arms, but I am held by God.

This burst of warmth and belonging and being known and held appeared like a surprise alley that led to an elaborate English garden on a cobblestone street. I was determined to head in one direction, and in my delay and ineptitude at getting there fast enough or at all, God had an alley for me. And the alley was wonderful.

It was Him.

The deepest longing of my heart: Him. His face staring into mine, His gentle composure and yet firm arms of strength, His whisper in my ear of all He sees, against all I feel I'm not.

God had something for me beyond the rim of my world, beyond my fence line. And it was Him.

It was all I've ever wanted but never knew to name.

I didn't know it could be this good.

We have a lot of surprise summer days in winter here in Missouri. It was sixty and sunny in January when we tromped out the door for our nine-thirty morning walk. We take the same route every day, the littles and I—the same half-mile loop through the nature preserve that borders our home. They see with new eyes every time. Today, one more Osage orange fell from the tree, and a new bird flitted in the brush. Raccoon tracks today, pressed down next to the deer tracks from yesterday. And, "Oh, is that a turkey running across the path?" It's their zoo, where the polar bear feels both familiar and wildly foreign every time you visit.

On this winter day, stripped of all that shrouds our view in spring and summer, the blackberry bushes were bare, as were the maples and black chestnuts. When most months of the year we can see only the path in front of us as we dodge errant tree limbs, on this day, we could see for what seemed like a mile. The warmth invited exploration.

We weaved in and around the path, finding a new waterfall we'd not seen before and one that might not be there again, the unique product of a downpour followed by freezing temps and then a flash of spring. Eventually, we landed in an area where the children had found home before. Trees battered by the wind and a large expanse without thick brush made the perfect combination for little explorers. On this day, we lingered extra long. I stood in one place, taking it all in. The children built "homes" out of twigs and leaves, and I watched the water at the creek, not them, feeling secure that the road was far from where they could walk, as was the turn of the creek. They were far from danger and full of possibility.

Their housebuilding continued, interrupted only by the curious search for animal bones. This was their Narnia, a world of their own that felt limitless, where children were sovereign and yet still subject to a hand of protection and guidance.

As I watched the water making a new path for itself through the creek bed, as it often does after a hard rain or thawing freeze, the thought came to me: *This is the boundaried but boundary-less life. This is a small picture of life in God.*

We fixate on our boundaries and limitations, such that we can't imagine a world that has His limitations (the ones we resent most) but also is without boundaries and full of beauty to explore. We struggle to imagine a life where God offers us exceedingly, abundantly all that we ask or imagine but also says no. This paradox confounds us. That He would answer no to the loudest cries of our hearts and yet open heaven to release blessings that we couldn't possibly conceive snaps the caution tape we put around our lives.

But this God—He is the God of paradox, the God who doesn't

heal your child but restores your relationship with your mom after you've stopped praying for restoration. God allows a ceiling on your work but makes your stagnant marriage come alive. God traps you in a city that you resent—you, the country girl—and in a church that feels dry, only to make your spiritual life thrive. You break your leg just at the start of training for a major race, and He gives you friends to rally around you when you aren't looking. You want healing for your body, and He heals a long-dark place in your heart.

The God of my children's wilderness—where they are architects, builders, explorers, and archaeologists—also surrounds their Narnia with a now-roaring creek to encircle them.

The paradox of God is that within the boundaries we resent there is a life that is limitless in Him. And we cannot see that limitlessness without the boundaries that we've been praying for decades would lift. When they don't move, we become more inclined to find Him within them.

"I didn't know it could be this good," I whispered to Nate, still unsure of my words.

We were walking through the lowest valley we'd known in years—one of our biggest fears—and after more than a year of grieving and many days when the clouds hung low over my head from morning until night, the circumstance for which we'd both prayed day and night still was not lifting. In fact, it looked worse. But something happened in the time when I'd permitted myself to grieve without a deadline—something otherworldly.

God felt palpable to me.

Many days while grieving, I felt like He was absent. I'd come to accept, as I leaned into others who experienced the kind of grief that we had, that God's mysterious absence was often a part of His way in grief. So I had stopped reaching for the warmth of His presence and settled myself in the comfort of His Word while feeling parented. Just like my nine-year-old, who can't understand why the teenagers can stay up late with their friends while he has a bedtime, I was at the mercy of God, my Dad.

I experienced a strange and growing acceptance as my dreams faded before my eyes. The grief became less something I fought or even endured and more something I welcomed like you might a friend as a houseguest: not wanting them to remain forever or creating a lifestyle around them but acknowledging that, for a time, there are gifts to be had by hosting them. And as I did this with grief, God came unexpectedly, as if to say, *Perhaps it's time for a rebuild of those dreams.*

I'd stopped asking for the dreams or even a rebuild of the dreams. I'd been through enough rotations of Friday's loss and Saturday's grief to know that the most freeing response was not to count the hours until Sunday's resurrection but to nestle myself inside of Saturday as a child who's young enough not to distinguish between whether it's four days or fourteen days until her birthday. I wanted all that His Saturday of grief held for me.

And Saturday held Him—His strong forearms, His firm grip, the assurances of Him I found in Scripture even when He seemed absent.

I wasn't moving from there until it was time.

And one day, it was time.

I woke to the clouds parting. Our circumstances hadn't shifted, but my heart felt a lifting. Perhaps a result of my accepting my boundary lines or just of His mysterious way, I felt a lifting.

The little things I'd noticed when the big thing felt so hard— Charlotte's raspy laugh, Nate's knowing way of looking at me,

Caleb's quick wit, the way our property staged both sunrise and sunset—now were in technicolor. They were no longer consolations to my grief but part of the prize. God had expanded me when I wasn't looking. I could hold things and new things and many things.

On the morning I whispered to Nate, as we talked about how somehow, in this brokenness in our circumstances, we were falling even more in love twenty-two years into marriage, "I didn't know it could be this good," I meant with him and in our marriage, but I also meant something bigger than that. I meant all of it. One of our biggest fears was occurring, yet God didn't require us to overcome it or make it not happen to find life.

"For whoever wants to save their life will lose it, but whoever loses their life for me will find it" (Matt. 16:25). Or as the New Living Translation puts it, "If you try to hang on to your life, you will lose it. But if you give up your life for my sake, you will save it."

By the grace of God, I stopped hanging on. Instead of scraping my shins trying to climb over the fence, I accepted that He had a life for me inside of it. I'd lost substantially, but then I found.

Life was beginning to look good. *So good*.

Instead of fighting fiercely to change it in prayer and action, I've accepted Friday's crossbeam, sat in the grief of Saturday's loss, and am now experiencing dozens of Sunday resurrections.

He takes us over the rim of the world, beyond what we might ask or imagine. This. *This* is a glimpse of God's exceeding abundance.

Can you imagine a world where, even at times, your fence cramps you and your dreams and your vision for your life even more than it does now, but you are okay? More than okay, you are alive inside the story God has given you.

The fence line has a purpose. It's not to be hurdled but to define the place within which we live out the story He has given us. The field in front of us is for pulling the dusty nets out of the garage and catching the butterflies that rest on the milkweed there. Make the grass our beds, stare into the cerulean sky, and watch for gulls over-head. The life out the back door, no matter how narrow and sparse it might feel, is the best life for finding Him.

And then when you least expect it, He says, *Let's take the road over the rim of our world.*

God is a dream maker.

And He is beautiful.

——— *For Your Continued Pursuit* ———

Genesis 8:22 | Exodus 33:11 | Numbers 6:24–26 | Psalm 10:17–18 | Psalm 16:6 | Psalm 27:4, 8 | Isaiah 33:17 | Joel 2:23–25 | Matthew 16:25 | 1 Corinthians 13:12 | Ephesians 3:20–21 | 1 John 3:2 | Revelation 22:4

Acknowledgments

"A bookseller," said Grandfather, "is the link between mind and mind, the feeder of the hungry, very often the binder up of wounds. There he sits, your bookseller, surrounded by a thousand minds all done up neatly in cardboard cases; beautiful minds, courageous minds, strong minds, wise minds, all sorts and conditions. A writer has to spin his work out of himself and the effect upon the character is often disastrous. It inflates the ego. Now your bookseller sinks his own ego in a thousand different egos that he introduces one to the other. Yes. . . . It's a great vocation. . . . Moreover his life is one of wide horizons. He deals in the stuff of eternity and there's no death in a bookseller's shop."

—ELIZABETH GOUDGE, *A City of Bells*

TO MY "BOOKSELLERS"—THE ONES WHO HAVE CARRIED these words from my mind and life to the "hungry": *thank you*.

Carly Kellerman, I am quite blessed by what a good fit it was for us to work together! Thank you for helping me speak clearly when I mumbled, bringing precision when I was foggy, and kneading this book until it became a work that I love. You became a mother of two while I wrote, and your "limitations" only served to enhance my work, proving true what I've written. Carolyn McCready, you inherited me and yet handled this message as if it were your own. I'm so grateful for your well-honed skill and the wisdom of years that you brought to my message. Brian Phipps, your attention to detail was critical to turning this manuscript into an experience for my readers. Alicia Kasen, you are one of the most enjoyable parts of a marketing process through which I (ahem) sometimes grit my teeth. The way you continue to champion the work of my heart will forever endear you to me. And Paul Fisher and Matt Bray, you've filled out this dream team. Jana Muntsinger and Pamela McClure, I squealed when they told me you'd be stewarding another one of my books. The delicacy and precision with which you handle your authors is rare—and needed. Tim Willard, your skill and passion for your craft spills over into the lives of your friends. Your instruction and your pep talks coached my heart as I wrote this book. GoldenRealm and Paravel Insights teams, I've spent many a date night hearing about each of you from Nate. What a gift now to have you in my corner and see for myself your talent and your hearts. Mike Salisbury (and team—Curtis and Karen Yates, you too), my big (little) brother, my pastor, my coach, thank you for your wisdom and your friendship. Dear "booksellers"—all of you whom I've just listed and more—this book was crafted and delivered by your hands as much as by mine.

To my internal team, also "booksellers": Jodi Schipper, you do your job with such excellence and yet your heart is not at risk while producing such stellar work. You are a rare combination of heart and hand. Erica Nork, it is no exaggeration to say I could not do this without you. You have become a sister to me and I will be forever grateful for your investment in this work and, really, in my life. Joy Turner, after more than a decade of working with you, I'm still in awe of your creativity, your humor, your intentionality, and the way you love people. Having you on my team (and also in my life) only makes us better. Ladies: you deal "in the stuff of eternity." So much of my joy in doing this work is working with each of you.

To the sages who are fifteen-ish years my senior, my "friend-tors": this book is what it is because of your wisdom and mentorship in my life. You didn't know it at the time, but you mentored this message. Lisa Jacobson, Barbara Rainey, Jodie Berndt, Sue Kawase, Susan Yates, Pam Bloom, Amy Loy, Alisa Keeton, Kristin Wall, Jina Patton, Jen Roberts, Cindy Finley, Julie Baker, and others I'm sure I've momentarily forgotten whose names will come to me at two o'clock in the morning the night after this book goes to print: your going before me in years and age and life and your own stories have made mine that much more bearable. Your well-earned grays are silver. Thank you for your vulnerability and your hand-holding.

To my prayer team: the time you spend in secret praying for my writing and these readers (and offering prayerful, thoughtful input on things like book covers and titles) adds a beauty to this work that only God truly sees. But I get a glimpse of it, and I know this book wouldn't be what it is without your hidden investment.

To Rick Pierce: your counsel to Nate and me has continued to grow our roots in God within our finitude (rather than fighting against it). Your life work is producing much fruit in our marriage and family.

And, oh, to my friends: I am so rich in friendship! During a year of great loss, each one of you has carried me at times when I thought I might sink. You know who you are—the girls huddling in my basement over Enjoy Pure Food dinners and laughter and tears, my dearest friends whose telephone lines are now Voxer (praise God for modern technology), the Sisterhood that Alyssa Bethke not so serendipitously gathered, House Church ladies and still (always) my

MT—I would not have made it this year of writing and hard living without you.

Karen Welter, my mom: you buoy me, over and over again, in this crazy life Nate and I have said yes to living. We roped you in, and you are all in.

Lily, Hope, Eden, Caleb, Bo, Virginia, and Charlotte—my most beautiful limitations: my prayer is that you may one day know how deep my affections run for each of you. Thank you for giving me a life such that I have words to write about subjects like this. I love you to the moon and back.

Nate: oh, babe, it just keeps getting better, this life with you. And I couldn't write a page of this without your bolstering—serving in the shadows when no one is looking. I feel more giddy about you today than I did at twenty-two. You are the man of my dreams, the ones unrealized at twenty-two, but lived today.

And, God—*Father*—my boundary-maker: I got to do this again with You. Thank You for giving me another story to tell, another reason to hold Your hand and write.

Every Bitter Thing Is Sweet

Tasting the Goodness of God in All Things

Sara Hagerty

Taste the Goodness of God in All Things

Sara Hagerty found Him when life stopped working for her. She found Him when she was a young adult mired in spiritual busyness and when she was a newlywed bride with doubts about whether her fledgling marriage would survive. She found Him alone in the night as she cradled her longing for babies who did not come. She found Him as she kissed the faces of children on another continent who had lived years without a mommy's touch.

In *Every Bitter Thing Is Sweet*, Hagerty weaves fabric from the narrative of her life into the mosaic of a Creator who mends broken stories. Here you will see a God who is present in every changing circumstance. Most significant, you see a God who is present in every unchanging circumstance as well.

Whatever lost expectations you are facing—in family, career, singleness, or marriage—*Every Bitter Thing Is Sweet* will bring you closer to a God who longs for you to know Him more.

Going beyond the narrative to offer timeless insight, Hagerty brings you back to hope, back to healing, back to a place that God is holding for you alone—a place where the unseen is more real than what the eye can perceive. A place where every bitter thing is sweet.

Adore

A Simple Practice for Experiencing God in the Middle Minutes of Your Day

Sara Hagerty

A simple, soul-nourishing practice for engaging with God in the middle minutes of your day.

None of us signed up for a conventional experience with the unconventional God, yet too often the spiritual life can become routine or, dare we say it, even boring.

For anyone who longs to experience God in the thick of life's demands, Sara Hagerty's *Adore* gives us all permission to admit "I barely know You, God." This honest admission is the first step closer to this familiar stranger. You'll learn the simple practice of adoration—of starting where you are and letting the grit of your day greet the beauty of God's presence.

Adoration is for the off moments and middle minutes. It's there for you when you feel rushed at 7:37 a.m. It's there when you feel over-crowded by your kids or coworkers at 12:17 p.m. It's there when you feel stuck and frustrated at 5:53 p.m. Adoration is the place where you put how you feel in front of God's Word and watch what happens to your insides. It's what you were made for.

Join Sara in this soul-stirring journey through thirty attributes of God that will help you hone the habit of adoration and see God with fresh eyes. Experience a new way of engaging with God in your everyday. *Adore* will show you how.

The nearness and tenderness of God will be so real to you as you read this book. Sara builds words in such a way it feels like God is so near as you read them.
>
> —Jennie Allen, author and founder of IF:Gathering

Available in stores and online!

Unseen

The Gift of Being Hidden in a World That Loves to Be Noticed

Sara Hagerty

Every heart longs to be seen and understood. Yet most of our lives is unwitnessed. We spend our days working, driving, parenting. We sometimes spend whole seasons feeling unnoticed and unappreciated. So how do we find contentment when we feel so hidden?

In *Unseen*, Sara Hagerty suggests that this is exactly what God intended. He is the only one who truly knows us. He is the only one who understands the value of the unseen in our lives. When this truth seeps into our souls, we realize that only when we hide ourselves in God can we give ourselves to others in true freedom and know the joy of a deeper relationship with the God who sees us.

Through an eloquent exploration of both personal and biblical story, Hagerty calls us to offer every unseen minute of our lives to God. God is in the secret places of our lives that no one else witnesses. But we've not been relegated to these places. We've been invited.

We may be "wasting" ourselves in a hidden corner today: The cubicle on the fourth floor. The hospital bedside of an elderly parent. The laundry room. But these are the places God uses to meet us with a radical love. These are the places that produce the kind of unhinged love in us that gives everything at His feet, whether or not anyone else ever proclaims our name, whether or not anyone else ever sees.

God's invitation is not just for a season or a day. It is the question of our lives: "When no one else applauds you, when it makes no sense, when you see no results will you waste your love on Me?"

Available in stores and online!

From the Publisher

GREAT BOOKS
ARE EVEN BETTER WHEN THEY'RE SHARED!

Help other readers find this one:

- Post a review at your favorite online bookseller

- Post a picture on a social media account and share why you enjoyed it

- Send a note to a friend who would also love it—or better yet, give them a copy

Thanks for reading!